What people are saying about the *Difficult Conversations* workshop:

"We came as a diverse group of leaders in government, business, nonprofit, and religious sectors. Even with our diversity, the workshop managed to speak directly to each individual and created a common language we can use when working together."
—Jesica Rhone, Director of International Programs, The McConnell Foundation

"It was amazing to see city leaders and the citizens they serve come together from all sides of the political spectrum — and across religious and socio-economic backgrounds — to learn how to work together for the good of our community. Kern is a steady, compassionate guide and an expert facilitator."
—Janessa Gans Wilder, Founder and CEO, Euphrates Institute

Difficult
Conversations

The Art and Science
of Working Together

KERN BEARE

POP THE BUBBLE PRESS

MOUNTAIN VIEW, CALIFORNIA

Printed in the United States of America.
ISBN: 978-1-7340458-0-2 (softcover)
ISBN: 978-1-7340458-1-9 (ebook)

Cover and interior design by Vicky Vaughn Shea, Ponderosa Pine Design
Cover and interior illustrations by Michelle Child
Author photo by Ashley Schmitz
Publishing consultant: Holly Brady, Brady New Media Publishing

Address permission requests to:
Pop the Bubble Press
662 Ehrhorn Avenue
Mountain View, CA 94041
info@popthebubble.org

For more information or to purchase multiple copies of this book at reduced prices, please inquire at info@popthebubble.org.

For more information on Difficult Conversations workshops, please visit www.difficultconversationsproject.org

For everyone who wants to learn to get along.

Virtually every spiritual tradition distinguishes the self-clinging ego from the deeper, creative Self: little self as opposed to big Self. The big Self is transpersonal, beyond any separated individuality, the common ground we all share.
— Stephen Nachmanovitch, musician and author

I know the world is bruised and bleeding, and though it is important not to ignore its pain, it is also critical to refuse to succumb to its malevolence. Like failure, chaos contains information that can lead to knowledge — even wisdom.
— Toni Morrison, author

Contents

Preface

*D*ifficult Conversations: The Art and Science of Working Together is based on a workshop I've been leading with diverse audiences around the country since the summer of 2017. I developed the workshop following a cross-country "conversation road tour" I took with my son just after the 2016 presidential election. We wanted to better understand what other people were thinking and feeling about the state of our country — and to discover how we might move forward together.

The conversations we had almost always surprised us. Like the pro-Trump Libertarian in Reno, Nevada, who told us that undocumented immigrants were tearing our country apart, and who later shared how he used to be anti-gay-marriage until a gay couple moved next door. The small circle of teachers from a community college in Bowling Green, Kentucky, who were in tears over the 2016 election, but who told us it's fear that fuels our national divide, and that we need to have compassion for one another. And the black Vietnam war vet we met in Birmingham, Alabama, on Martin Luther King Jr. Day who told us that his wife lost her sister and her eye in the 1963 bombing of the 16th Street Baptist Church, and then shared that the only way to move forward was with love and forgiveness.

These and many other conversations gave us much to think about as we drove often long distances between each scheduled stop. And in the evening, we'd think about them again as we transcribed, edited, and posted the conversations on our blog.

By the end of our tour we felt like we'd learned something. The conversations took us beneath the surface of our divide to its deeper currents, where it was possible to see how we, as a country, might move forward. Here are three of our most important insights:

- **It's about relationship.** Yes, our economic, social, and political divisions are real. But they're symptoms of a deeper problem: our disconnection from one another. For various reasons and in various ways, we've all retreated inside bubbles too small for today's complex, challenging, and interconnected world. More than ever, we need to "pop our bubbles" to expand our connections and perspectives.

- **People want to talk.** The hostile diatribes and intransigent perspectives people post on social media are not what we found when meeting face to face. Yes, liberals are upset, but more than that, they want to understand and build bridges. Conservatives, too, want to talk, but may be reticent for fear of being vilified for their point of view. We have to learn how to create spaces for respectful dialogue so that we can begin the process of finding, and building on, common ground.

- **We need new skills.** To heal our nation and move forward together, we need to master some radical new ways of being and relating. No longer can we reserve the right to vilify or dehumanize "the other." Turning people into enemies who need to be marginalized or vanquished does nothing but deepen our divide. Only by standing together on the ground of our common humanity can we secure the future we most want for our children and ourselves.

The workshop and this book — *Difficult Conversations: The Art and Science of Working Together* — are outcomes of our journey and responses to these three insights.

Introduction

According to a recent survey, if you're a democrat, there's a 60 percent chance that you view the Republican Party as a threat to the United States, and a 40 percent chance that you regard it as "downright evil." If you're a republican, the same odds apply to your perceptions of the Democratic Party.[1]

These are telling statistics, a warning that we've lit a fire under our divisive tribal tendencies and put our democracy at risk. More than that, we've put all future generations at risk by failing to come together to address our critical social, economic, and environmental challenges.

Difficult Conversations: The Art and Science of Working Together offers a framework for finding common ground and healing our divide. It does this by offering a new set of "survival strategies" that counter the instinctual fight, flee, or freeze survival drive reaction that difficult conversations often trigger:

- **Fight.** We argue our point aggressively in an effort to "win."
- **Flee.** We avoid or give up on the conversation altogether.
- **Freeze.** We find ourselves flustered, unable to respond at all.

The premise of this book is that these fight/flee/freeze

1

instincts developed early in our evolution when the most important survival skill was to avoid getting eaten. They're completely inappropriate, however, for responding to the challenges of today, when the most important survival skill is *cooperation*. For these challenges, we need a new set of survival strategies.

Here, in brief, are the three strategies we'll be exploring:

- **Prioritize the relationship over being right.**
  Research shows that our fight/flee/freeze survival drive is often triggered when someone challenges our deeply held beliefs. Research also shows that when that happens, we lose a host of cognitive capacities that are at the heart of being human, including empathy, moral reasoning and even intuition. Bereft of these capacities, the conversation — and sometimes the relationship itself — typically comes to an unsatisfying and even ugly end.

  It doesn't have to be this way. Evidence abounds that differences in values, attitudes, and beliefs become far less significant when a deeper basis of relationship is formed — especially when it's rooted in our common humanity. In this book you'll learn strategies for building such relationships, in turn strengthening the critical capacities you need for creative engagement.

- **See beyond your story.** Most of us have the (often unconscious) assumption that our "story" — the particular set of life experiences from which we derive our sense of self — is the totality of who we are. This merging of "self" and "story" explains one of the most surprising findings of neurobiology: threats to our story-self — to our values, attitudes and beliefs — activate the same parts of our brain as threats to our physical self, triggering our fight, flee, or freeze reactions. When this happens, simmering disagreements can quickly become combustible.

  At the same time, we're learning that our identity encompasses far more than our story. Studies show that a more expanded sense of self emerges when we "switch off" our story-self, unleashing a host of positive emotions and attributes. These include joy, compassion, gratitude, flexibility, creativity and receptivity to new ideas — all of which counteract our survival drive instinct. In this book you'll learn more about this "expanded self" and how to access its capacities.

- **Transform resistance into response.** Resistance is our early-warning system that our survival drive is beginning to kick into gear. When we're in resistance, our attention narrows, our heart rate increases, and our stress levels rise — all signals of an emerging fight, flee, or freeze reaction. In this book you'll learn about the neuropsychology of resistance, why transforming our resistance into response strengthens our cognitive capacities, and how the brain has evolved to actually help us undergo this transformative process.

As you'll see, taken together, these three new survival strategies unleash the very capacities we need to heal our current divide. They do this, in part, by resetting and enlarging the context within which we see our self, and our relationship to one another — two critical shifts in perspective that reveal the common ground on which we stand, and that give us the means to continue pursuing the vision upon which this nation was built: *out of many, one.*

How to Use This Book

This book follows the flow of my workshop and includes many of the same suggested activities. To get the most out of the book, I strongly recommend you complete the activities. The personal reflections you're asked to make are especially integral to the experience and build on one another. You'll start by identifying a difficult conversation in your life, and then see how the principles and strategies from each chapter can be applied to that conversation.

To further enrich your experience with the book, and to more closely simulate the workshop's interactive environment, consider forming a book group, and gathering once a week to share your reflections from the previous week's reading.

There are two media pieces I use in my workshop that are also integral to the flow of the book. I've done my best to capture in written form the essence of these pieces, but if you're able, a better alternative is to experience them directly. You can find them on my Vimeo channel (https://vimeo.com/difficultconversations/), along with other recommended media that support the content of the book.

If you have any comments or questions about the book or the workshop, you can contact me through my website: http://www.difficultconversationsproject.org/.

1   N. Kalmoe & L. Mason, "Lethal Mass Partisanship: Prevalence, Correlates, and Electoral Contingencies" (paper presented at the annual meeting of the American Political Science Association, Boston, MA, Aug. 30-Sept. 2, 2018).

1

The Science of Difficult Conversations

Alligators do not come when they are called. Some kind of leash to control the reptile brain is necessary.

— George Vaillant, Psychoanalyst and Research Psychiatrist, Harvard University

There's an audiotape I often play at the beginning of my Difficult Conversations workshop — a real-life conversation between two women on opposite sides of the abortion debate.

The women meet under contentious circumstances: a pro-life rally and a pro-choice counter rally. The two warring tribes are facing off on opposite sides of the street, each inciting the other with provocative signs and verbal bomb-throwing. The atmosphere is tense.

The woman on the pro-life side, recognizing that yelling "doesn't change hearts and minds," makes the first move. She invites the woman on the pro-choice side to talk.

A reporter is there to capture the conversation, enticed by this unusual attempt to bridge the divide.

The conversation plays out in just under five minutes, and as you listen you feel hopeful. In counterpoint to the surrounding maelstrom, the two women are civil to each other, even kind. The pro-life woman, forgoing the familiar talking points, begins by sharing a personal story, perhaps hoping it will help the other woman better understand her perspective. But it's only partially effective. While the pro-choice woman graciously acknowledges the story, she almost immediately shifts into sharing her own point of view. Soon an all-too-familiar pattern is established: the combative tit-for-tat of opposing facts, experiences, and priorities.

To the women's credit they're never mean-spirited. But within minutes their attempted dialogue becomes two overlapping and competing monologues. Deafened by the rising volume of their own intermingled voices, they finally (and politely) decide to end their conversation and return to their respective tribes.

I play this audiotape not to launch into a difficult conversation on abortion, but rather to consider the

LISTEN

You can listen to the actual five-minute conversation between these two women at the abortion rally on my Vimeo channel. Go to https://vimeo.com/difficultconversations/. Click on the first video, "Dialogue or Debate."

conversation itself as a case study. What exactly made this conversation difficult, and what could either woman have done to produce a better outcome for both?

When I ask these questions in the workshop, the answers I get typically focus on the women's behavior. What made the conversation difficult was their failure to listen to one another. What would have made it better is if they'd taken the time to ask clarifying questions; to seek to understand not only what the other person thought or believed, but also *why*.

These are solid answers, and they're backed by research that shows that when people feel heard and understood, they become less rigid in their thinking and more open to new ideas.[1]

But here's the conundrum: If we know the prescription for a better conversation, why don't more of us follow it? What makes listening to people we disagree with so difficult that we act in ways we know are counterproductive?

Difficult Conversations Trigger Our Survival Drive

The answer, it turns out, has to do with some very ancient human programming. Attitudes and beliefs we find threatening often trigger our survival drive: a powerful set of primitive, instinctual reactions we know as "fight, flee or freeze" (the "three Fs"). Adapted to the world of conversation, the three Fs typically look like this:

- **Fight.** We argue our point aggressively in an effort

to *win* the argument.

- **Flee.** We avoid or give up on the conversation and retreat to the security and comfort of our "tribe."
- **Freeze.** Dumbstruck by some unexpected turn in the conversation, we fail to muster any kind of response at all.

Now, if our goal is to build bridges and find common ground, it's pretty clear these survival drive strategies have limited to no applicability. So why do we succumb to them? Why does an instinct originally intended to help us survive an encounter with a hungry lion take control when we're confronted with a difficult conversation?

The reason is simple but also pretty shocking: according to neuroscience, whether it's threatening lions or threatening ideas, *our brain can't tell the difference.* Both activate the brain's fear center, which in turn triggers our survival drive.[2]

In other words, as far as our brain is concerned, a threat to our beliefs is just another kind of lion, waiting to devour us.

Here's a simplified description of how it works:

Tucked within our lower brain is an almond-shaped cluster of neurons called the amygdala. Associated with fear and strong emotion, the amygdala is part of the brain's neural "fear circuit," charged with registering threats and, if necessary, ramping up our fight/flee/freeze reaction.

Fight, Flee or Freeze? The Gym Story

I was at the gym, riding on a stationary bicycle and watching on the built-in TV monitor one of those endless cable news programs — call it "News Network A." On the bike next to me was a man watching a different channel. After chatting in a friendly way, he leaned over to see what I was watching. "Oh, News Network A!" he said. "It's so biased."

His comment surprised but didn't offend me. I actually agree that News Network A is biased. But then I looked over to see what *he* was watching and discovered it was the equally biased "News Network B." I turned away and said, dismissively, "They're *all* biased!" And I stopped talking to him.

His inability to see the bias of his own preferred news channel somehow crossed a line for me. Rather than engage to see what possibilities might emerge to expand his thinking — and my own — I instead chose to "flee" into my own little world, cutting off any further communication.

Not a proud moment!

But the amygdala is also connected to another neural circuit, one that's part of the upper brain's "executive center": the medial prefrontal cortex (mPFC). When a threat is detected, one role of the mPFC is to determine if the amygdala is responding appropriately or overreacting. (Is that a burglar in the closet? Or just my kid playing hide-and-seek?)

If the response is appropriate, the mPFC sits back and lets the amygdala amp up our survival drive unimpeded until the danger has passed. If it's not appropriate — if the amygdala has pushed the panic button prematurely — the mPFC modulates or extinguishes the amygdala's survival drive so that we (quite literally) regain our senses, preventing us from taking actions we'll later regret.

Now here's the critical part: for all this to go smoothly, a strong neural connection between the amygdala and the mPFC is essential. And this is where things can go wrong.

If — for reasons we'll get to later in the book — our amygdala overreacts to a perceived threat ("overheats" with fear, anger, or other negative emotion), critical neural connections between our lower limbic brain and our medial prefrontal cortex can weaken, preventing the mPFC from playing its modulating role. This can cause us — in the words of Daniel J. Siegel, founding director of the Mindful Awareness Research Center at UCLA— to "flip our lid": our negative emotions run so hot that the connection to our mPFC breaks down, disabling our executive-level cognitive

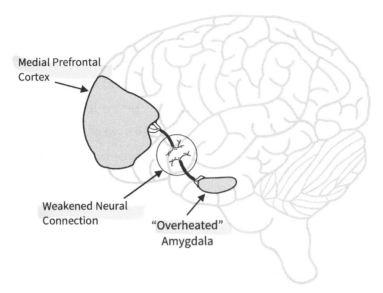

Conceptual illustration of "flipping our lid": When our amygdala overheats with negative emotions, we weaken the connection to our medial prefrontal cortex and lose critical cognitive capabilities.

functions. "Road rage" is one well-known example of "flipping our lid."

Why does this matter? Here's a list of the major, critical cognitive capabilities we lose when we "flip our lid":

- compassion;
- emotional balance;
- response flexibility;
- empathy;
- self-knowing awareness;
- fear modulation/fear extinction;
- intuition;
- moral reasoning.

WATCH

For a quick synopsis of the science behind "flipping our lid," check out "Hand Model of the Brain," a short video with noted neuropsychiatrist Daniel J. Siegel, on my Vimeo channel at https://vimeo.com/difficultconversations/.

No wonder difficult conversations are difficult! Once our survival drive is triggered, we've lost the very capacities we need to engage in the conversation compassionately, creatively, and productively.

So, to recap . . .

We react to threats to our deeply held beliefs as if they were threats to our physical body, triggering our survival drive. But this fight/flee/freeze instinct — "only modestly more sophisticated than an alligator's"[3]— developed early in our evolution when the most important survival skill was *to avoid getting eaten*. It's a completely inappropriate instinct for responding to the challenges of today, where the most important survival skill is *cooperation*.

So, what can we do? Is it possible to disentangle our deeply held beliefs from this ancient survival drive? Can we learn to stay in the conversation without losing the critical cognitive capabilities we need to collectively address the challenges of today's world? Can we learn to stay present and creative so that our interactions are at worst civil, and at best transformational?

Research and experience tell us the answer is unequivocally *yes*. But it requires an entirely different set of survival strategies, which we explore in the following chapters.

A Common Objection

At this point in the workshop, someone usually observes that certain attitudes and beliefs do indeed threaten our physical survival: for example, people who are hostile toward a particular racial, ethnic, or religious group (or, these days, even someone's political ideology). In these situations, isn't our instinctive survival drive — ancient or not — still appropriate?

It's an important question, and addressing it helps clarify my point. Clearly such threats do exist. The question is whether our survival drive — fight, flee or freeze — offers a sufficient and effective response *to* those threats. The premise of this book is that the answer is *no*. In fact, it only makes things worse.

As mentioned, the three Fs evolved for situations involving a sudden and immediate threat to life and limb. For example, a tiger that's about to eat us, a rock that's about to fall on us, or a car that's about to run over us. In these instances, pausing to reflect on the best course of action is clearly counter to our self-interest. Choose to delay in situations like these and you're a goner.

But if we want to figure out how to mitigate the *ongoing risks* posed by tigers, rocks, and cars, we need strategies that operate within a longer time horizon, strategies that call on our ability to think creatively and empathically.

The Triune Brain

One simple, but useful model of the brain highlights its three major structures:

1. The brainstem (sometimes called the "reptilian" brain), which monitors basic physiological processes such breathing, heart rate, and blood pressure. Working in tandem with our limbic system and neocortex, it's also charged with registering threats and triggering our fight/flee/freeze survival drive.

2. The limbic system (sometimes called the "emotional" brain), which "synthesizes" information from the brainstem and facilitates "the integration of a wide range of basic mental processes, such as the

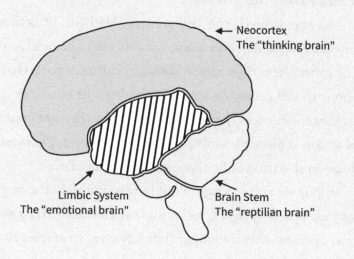

← Neocortex
The "thinking brain"

Limbic System
The "emotional brain"

Brain Stem
The "reptilian brain"

appraisal of meaning, the processing of social signals, and the activation of emotion."[1] (The amygdala, which we talked about earlier, is nestled inside the limbic system.)

3. The neocortex (sometimes called the "rational" or "thinking" brain), which, as we've already seen, is responsible for "more complex information processing functions such as perception, thinking, and reasoning."[2] The neocortex also includes the newest part of our brain, the *prefrontal* cortex, which is involved in integrating the functions of the cortex, the limbic system, and the brain stem. When we "flip our lid," it's the integrating function of the prefrontal cortex that's lost. We become "dis-integrated."

Note: For the purposes of this book, I refer to the brainstem and limbic system together as the "lower" brain, while the neocortex refers to the "upper" brain.

---

1   Daniel J. Siegel, *The Developing Mind: How Relationships and the Brain Interact to Shape Who We Are*, 2nd ed. (New York: Guilford Publications, 2012), 18.
2   Ibid.

None of these strategies are found within the domain of our survival drive. As Harvard psychoanalyst George Vaillant puts it:

> *Negative emotions are often crucial for survival— but only in time present. The positive emotions are more expansive and help us to broaden and build. They widen our tolerance, expand our moral compass, and enhance our creativity. They help us to survive in time future.*[4]

Threats rooted in ignorance, intolerance, and fear especially call for longer-term strategies. For millennia we've tried to avoid (flee), deny (freeze) or forcefully suppress (fight) these threats, with little to show for it. At best, we push them underground where they later re-emerge with great force and consequence (as is all too clear today).

I find the First Law of Thermodynamics to be instructive here: *energy* — and ignorance, intolerance, and fear are forms of energy — *cannot be created or destroyed; only transformed*. And the way to transform ignorance, intolerance, and fear is through creative engagement that fosters relationship-building and compassionate education, as the stories that follow illustrate.

Personal Assessment #1

Before proceeding, and to get the most out of our explora-
tion of the art and science of difficult conversations, take a
moment to think of a difficult conversation in your life. In a
notebook, answer the following questions:

- Who's involved?
- What's the subject?
- What specifically makes this difficult conversation
  difficult?

1   G. Bruneau and Rebecca Saxe, "The Power of Being Heard: The Benefits
of 'Perspective-Giving' in the Context of Intergroup Conflict," *Journal of
Experimental Social Psychology* 48, no 4, (July 2012), 855–866.
2   Jonas T. Kaplan, Sarah I. Gimbel & Sam Harris, "Neural Correlates of
Maintaining One's Political Beliefs in the Face of Counterevidence." *Scientific
Reports* 6, article 39589 (2016).
3   George Vaillant, *Spiritual Evolution: A Scientific Defense of Faith*, (New
York: Potter/TenSpeed/Harmony, 2008), 160.
4   Ibid., 5.

2

The New Survival Drive

Suprainstinctual survival strategies generate
something probably unique to humans: a moral point
of view that, on occasion, can transcend the interests
of the immediate group.
— Antonio R. Damasio, neurologist and author

Is it really possible to stay creatively engaged in a difficult conversation, one where our most precious beliefs and values are being challenged, without triggering our ancient fight, flee, or freeze survival drive? Can we really stay civil, constructive, and compassionate even with those who hold views that run counter to our own well-being?

And if it's possible, how do we do it?

To answer those questions, a good place to start is with the story of Megan Phelps-Roper, a former member of the famously anti-Semitic and homophobic Westboro Baptist Church.

Born into Westboro's presumptive "first family" (her

grandfather was the church's founder), Megan absorbed the cult's ideology virtually intravenously. By age five she was already traveling with her family to attend staged protests against gays and Jews, holding in her tiny hands picket signs she couldn't read: *Gays are Worthy of Death!* and *Your Rabbi is a Whore!* In 2009 Megan — now a tech-savvy millennial in her 20s — added a new tool to her proselytizing toolkit: she became the face and voice of Westboro on Twitter and other social media outlets, trolling for people to rebuke, influence, and convert.

But a funny thing happened on the way to the Twitterverse. She experienced something she never had before: a civil dialogue with the very people she'd been taught were the devil's disciples. Here's a lightly edited version of how she tells the story in her viral 2017 TED talk:

> *Initially, the people I encountered on the platform were the digital version of the screaming hordes I'd been seeing at protests since I was a kid. But in the midst of that digital brawl, a strange pattern developed. Someone would arrive at my profile with the usual rage and scorn; I would respond with a custom mix of Bible verses, pop culture references, and smiley faces. They would be understandably confused and caught off guard, but then a conversation would ensue. And it was civil — full of genuine curiosity on both sides. How had the other come to such outrageous conclusions about the world?*

Several of these online encounters eventually "bled into real life," including coming face to face with David, a Jew from Jerusalem.

People I'd sparred with on Twitter would come out to the picket line to see me when I protested in their city. A man named David was one such person. He ran a blog called "Jewlicious," and after several months of heated but friendly arguments online, he came out to see me at a picket in New Orleans. He brought me a Middle Eastern dessert from Jerusalem . . . and I brought him kosher chocolate and held a God hates Jews sign. There was no confusion about our positions, but the line between friend and foe was becoming blurred. We'd started to see each other as human beings, and it changed the way we spoke to one another.

Over time, the power of these interactions had a profound impact.

It took time, but eventually these conversations planted seeds of doubt in me. My friends on Twitter took the time to understand Westboro's doctrines, and in doing so, they were able to find inconsistencies I'd missed my entire life. Why did we advocate the death penalty for gays when Jesus said, "Let he who is without sin cast the first stone"? How could we claim to love our neighbors while at the same time praying for God to destroy them? The truth is that the care shown to me by these strangers on the Internet was itself a contradiction. It was growing evidence that people on the other side were not the demons I'd been led to believe.

As Megan's seeds of doubt grew, they eroded her trust in her church and eventually made it impossible for her to stay. *In spite of overwhelming grief and terror, I left Westboro in 2012.*

Megan's is an extraordinarily hopeful story, and as we'll see later, it's not unique — all the more reason to take a closer look. What was at work in these interactions on Twitter and in real life that led to this life-altering impact?

At the end of her TED talk, Megan offers her own assessment: four things her friends did differently that made real conversation possible.

- **Don't assume bad intent.** *Assuming ill motives almost instantly cuts us off from truly understanding why someone does and believes as they do. We forget that they're human beings with a lifetime of experience that shaped their minds. We get stuck on that first wave of anger, and the conversation has a very hard time ever moving beyond it. But when we assume good or neutral intent, we give our minds a much stronger framework for dialogue.*

- *Ask questions.* When we engage people across ideological divides, asking questions helps us map the disconnect between our differing points of view. . . . But asking questions [also] serves another purpose: it signals to someone that they're being heard. When my friends on Twitter stopped accusing and started asking questions, I almost automatically mirrored them. . . . It fundamentally changed the dynamic of our conversation.

- *Stay calm.* When my husband was still just an anonymous Twitter acquaintance, our discussions frequently became hard and pointed, but we always refused to escalate. Instead, he would change the subject. He would tell a joke or recommend a book or gently excuse himself from the conversation. We knew the discussion wasn't over, just paused for a time to bring us back to an even keel.

- *Make the argument.* As kind as my friends on Twitter were, if they hadn't actually made their arguments, it would've been so much harder for me to see the world in a different way. We are all a product of our upbringing, and our

WATCH

I recommend watching Megan's entire 15-minute TED talk. You can find it at www. TED.com. Search for the video by its title, "I Grew Up in the Westboro Baptist Church. Here's Why I Left."

beliefs reflect our experiences. We can't expect others
to spontaneously change their own minds. If we want
change, we have to make the case for it.

Going Deeper

Once again, we have an articulation of wise and helpful
strategies for engaging in true dialogue. And once again,
we all know how incredibly difficult these strategies can be
to execute. The first three in particular — *don't assume bad
intent, ask questions* and *stay calm* — collide head-on with
the knee-jerk instinct of our fight/flee/freeze survival drive.

So, let's take the analysis a little deeper. *Why* weren't
Megan's Twitter friends triggered by her outrageous and
harmful views? What gave them the ability to override
their survival drive and access these more effective ways
of relating — especially David, a Jew, and therefore a
direct target of Megan's toxic worldview? If anyone had
a reason to vilify and denounce Megan, it would be him.
What allowed him to not "flip his lid," and instead keep his
whole brain in the game, so that he could keep the dialogue
moving in a positive direction?

In pondering these questions for myself, I came to the
following conclusion: I believe David was able to override
his instinctual survival drive because somehow he knew
that, in this situation, *it didn't actually serve his survival.*
This is an essential point. We'll never give up the old for

the new if we feel the old is still working.

What life experiences might have led him to that insight, we can only guess. Perhaps he'd seen enough evidence in his life that turning people into enemies who need to be marginalized, defeated, or even eliminated only sustains and deepens the cycle of division and violence. Perhaps, too, he'd come to understand that in the end we humans are all in this together, and that our survival is a cooperative rather than a combative enterprise.

Whatever the reasons, I believe that this insight — that in the realm of human relations, our survival drive instinct runs counter to our individual and collective well-being — led David to new and more appropriate survival strategies in his interactions with Megan, strategies that would allow him to stay present, keep his whole brain in the game, and creatively work through the inevitable tensions and conflicts that would arise.

I don't know if David thinks in terms of possessing different survival strategies, or how he would describe them if he did. But as I've reflected on the model that he and many others have provided, together with what we're learning about human behavior from both the hard and soft sciences, I believe the following is a reasonable and useful articulation of what they might be:

- Prioritize the relationship over being right.
- See beyond your "story."
- Transform resistance into response.

Exploring these new survival strategies — and how they can help us seize the gifts of our differences, affirm our common humanity, and move us forward in unity — is the subject of the rest of this book.

3

New Survival Strategy #1:

Prioritize the Relationship Over Being Right

To put it simply, human connections

shape neural connections.

— Daniel J. Siegel, *The Developing Mind*

If you think about it, our first new survival drive strategy — *prioritize the relationship over being right* — is completely logical if our intention is to heal our divisions and find common ground. By putting the relationship first — by putting people before positions, connection before convictions — we have the best chance of establishing open channels of communication so that real dialogue can occur. After all, there's a lot of truth to the saying, "I won't care what you know until I know that you care."

But to be clear, putting the relationship first does not mean *abandoning* our position or convictions. The people who engaged Megan Phelps-Roper never changed their view that what she was doing as part of the Westboro Baptist Church was wrong and hateful. But they kept the relationship intact because they knew that was the only way she'd ever be open to their point of view. That's why, when things got heated, her friends would back off, change the subject, make jokes, and ask questions to get to know her better outside the context of her specific beliefs. As Megan observed in her TED talk, "We knew the discussion wasn't over, just paused for a time to bring us back to an even keel."

It's hard to argue with the logic of that approach. Rupture the relationship and you rupture the channels of communication. Nurture the relationship and you create the best opportunity for everyone to learn and change.

But there's another, even more powerful reason to put relationships first: it's how we all become more human. Literally.

Human Connections Shape Neural Connections

In the first chapter we saw how difficult conversations trigger our fight/flee/freeze survival drive and weaken the neural connections between our upper and lower brain, causing us to "flip our lid." We also saw that when that happens, we lose a number of crucial cognitive capabilities, including:

- compassion;
- emotional balance;
- response flexibility;
- empathy;
- self-knowing awareness;
- fear modulation/fear extinction;
- intuition;
- moral reasoning.

It's not much of an exaggeration to say that when we "flip our lid," we're pretty much out half a brain. We've severed the connections to our thinking/reasoning upper brain and left our reactive/emotional lower brain in charge — in the process undermining one of the most significant advances in human evolution. Let me explain what I mean, and how it relates to our first new survival strategy.

One of life's great mysteries is why human beings have such a large brain — about three times larger than our body mass alone would justify. What led to this development?

One generally accepted theory is that rising evolutionary pressures — including, ironically enough, climate change — required a matching increase in certain social and cognitive capabilities.[1] Presto: larger brain.

But *in what ways* did our brain get bigger? What specifically needed beefing up to give us our new and improved survival skills? Part of the answer is simply the addition of raw processing power in the form of a few billion more neurons, or what's called *grey matter*. But the more significant addition — particularly in the newest part of our brain, the prefrontal cortex — appears to be an increase in the connective tissue *between* the neurons, or what's called *white matter*. As Harvard psychiatrist George Vaillant explains:

> *From an evolutionary standpoint, the human frontal lobes are no different from those of chimpanzees in terms of number of neurons. Rather, it is the frontal lobe white matter, the connectivity between neurons through myelinated fibers, that accounts for the larger frontal lobes of humans.*[2]

So, here's the takeaway: when it comes to meeting increasingly complex challenges, sheer numbers of neurons only get us so far. After that, it's interconnectivity — neural integration — that unlocks the social and cognitive capacities we need to survive and thrive. And if increased neural integration was needed to meet the challenges of a few hundred thousand years ago, it's reasonable to assume increased neural integration is even more needed now.

Which brings us back to our first new survival strategy. Because what promotes neural integration? *Strong, resilient human relationships.*

Neuropsychiatrist Daniel J. Siegel suggests that when we prioritize the relationship, when we pause a difficult conversation in order to re-establish a positive connection with "the other," we stimulate in our own brain "the activity and growth of fibers that are integrative." And that gives us something he calls "response flexibility"— the ability to regulate our emotional state so that we can take in the bigger picture and perceive new options. Siegel puts it this way:

> *Intimate, reciprocal human communication may*
> *directly activate the neural circuitry responsible for*
> *giving meaning, responding flexibly, and shaping*
> *the subjective experience of an emotionally vibrant*
> *life. The basic idea is this: integrative communication*
> *leads to the growth of integrative fibers in the brain.* [3]

In other words, says Siegel, "interpersonal integration" — strong, resilient relationships — "facilitates neural integration."

Think about it. When we're able to get a broken relationship back on an even keel, our whole body responds positively. Our heart rate goes down, our stress levels subside, we breathe more easily, our lower and upper brain reconnect, our higher cognitive processes come back online, and we start thinking more clearly.

Contrast that outcome to how we feel when we hold onto our anger, our critical judgments, our resentment.

Contrast it to how we feel when we repeatedly re-live some offending or hurtful conversation in our head, wishing we had said this or done that — only to painfully remember that wishing cannot change what actually happened.

And finally, contrast it to how we feel every time we encounter a person we're in conflict with on the street, at the store, (in the gym!) — and instead of a friendly acknowledgment, we avert our gaze and pretend we don't see the other.

All these scenarios exact a heavy price: they weaken our brain's crucial "integrative fibers," which in turn weakens the fibers of our relationships and our communities — diminishing our collective capacity for creativity, compassion, and collaboration.

By now I hope I've made my point: *prioritizing the relationship over being right* is not just a nice or even noble idea. It's a process for bootstrapping our personal and collective evolution, essential for meeting the challenges of our increasingly complex world.

So, what then can we do? What does prioritizing the relationship look like? What are the strategies and tools that will help us achieve greater integration, personally and collectively?

Strategies for Reconnecting with Others

Reconnecting a stressed relationship — and consequently reconnecting a stressed brain — isn't easy. It takes commitment. Which in turn means being convinced, like Megan's friend David, that our survival-drive reaction is actually

How It Feels to Let Go of Our Argument

A t first glance, this first new survival strategy may seem like a paradox: *to make the best case for our position, we must be willing to let go of our position, if only momentarily.*

Even if we accept this paradox as logical, choosing not to defend a closely held belief or opinion can feel like the scary, weightless, lose-your-life drop of a high-speed rollercoaster ride. Even though we know things smooth out ahead, in the midst of the drop it's hard to shake the feeling that we're doing something foolish.

We're not. What we need to remember is that the voice in us that objects is coming from the old, reptilian part of our brain that should have no say in situations for which it was not designed. That part of our brain is all about zero-sum thinking, about not getting eaten by the tiger in the wild. It's an I-win-you-lose, my-gain-is-your-loss view of the world.

When we're trapped in that kind of thinking, prioritizing the relationship over being right can feel like being on the losing end of a zero-sum game. But the challenges we face today are non-zero-sum: we all *win* or we all lose. In a non-zero-sum world, my gain is your gain, and helping you helps me, too.

counter to our true survival interests. If we're clear on that, the following strategies can be helpful.

I'll start with a few simple suggestions I came across while researching material for my workshop, and then I'll get to what I consider "the mother of all reconnecting strategies."

- **Calm Down.** The first step when we find we're getting upset and we're in danger of "flipping our lid" is to make a conscious effort to calm down. One sequence of actions for doing so is called "PBS." It stands for:

  - Pause. Pause the conversation. Put it on hold. If necessary, remove yourself from the situation; take a walk and spend some time alone.

  - Breathe. Take a deep breath. You want to get oxygen back into your brain so you can start thinking again. A useful technique, scientifically documented, is to breathe in for a count of four, and out for a count of six. (Note: apparently, it's most effective if you breathe in and out through your nose.)

  - Smile. Research shows smiling has huge personal and interpersonal benefits:

    - It activates the release of neuropeptides that help fight off stress (neuropeptides are tiny molecules that allow neurons to communicate).

Give It Five Minutes

In his wonderful book *How to Think: A Survival Guide for a World at Odds*, Alan Jacobs tells a story that highlights the value of "calming down."

A man at a conference was listening to a talk and heard something to which he strenuously objected. When the talk was over, the man rushed up to the speaker and expressed his disagreement. The speaker listened to his objections and then advised the man to "give it five minutes."

The advice caught the man off guard, but later the wisdom of it sank in. He realized that once he heard something he disagreed with, he stopped listening to everything else the speaker said. As Jacobs tells it, the man had entered "Refutation Mode — and in Refutation Mode there is no listening. Moreover, when there is no listening, there is no thinking. To enter Refutation Mode is to say, in effect, that you've already done all the thinking you need to do, that no further information or reflection is required."[1]

The next time you find yourself in Refutation Mode, consider giving it five minutes and using the time to keep listening.

1 Alan Jacobs, *How to Think: A Survival Guide for a World at Odds* (New York: Currency Publications, 2017), 8.

- It releases your feel-good neurotransmitters: dopamine, endorphins and serotonin. These relax your body, lower your heart rate and blood pressure, and lift your mood.
- It has a positive impact on the people around you. Seeing a smiling face activates our orbito-frontal cortex, the brain region that processes sensory rewards. When you view a person smiling, you actually feel rewarded!

- **Re-engage.** Once we've calmed down, the next step is to re-engage in a way that gets the conversation back on track. Here are strategies the experts swear by. I call these the "Three A's":
  - Appreciate. Find something about the other person to appreciate. This evokes positive emotions in both of you.
  - Agree. Find something in the other's perspective you can agree with. Being agreed with stimulates the reward centers of our brain, releasing oxytocin — known as the "love hormone."
  - Articulate. Take time to articulate the other's perspective. This is particularly effective at building trust and good will. (My friend, a professional mediator, calls this a magical tool.)

There's one more "A" word I want to add to the list:

- **Apologize.** If you've done something worth apologizing for, apologize. It works wonders. Admitting our mistakes makes us more humble and more relatable. It also makes the other person feel better respected and therefore more kindly toward us.

Looping for Understanding

Another engagement technique, related to our third "A" (Articulate the other's perspective) is called "looping for understanding." Often we assume we've understood what another has said, but as we'll see later on, we have so many filters through which we interpret the world, most of the time we get it wrong. Looping for understanding means you keep feeding back what the other has said until they say you've heard it right. In yet another technique that takes it a step further: you keep looping until you convey the other's point of view not only in words, but also with emotional resonance. It's the difference between parroting another's perspective and truly understanding it.

The Power of Apology: The Bartender Story

My wife and I walked into a crowded restaurant. No tables were available, so we took our dinner at the bar. We sat there quite a while, waiting to be noticed by the bartender, and I started  to get upset at being ignored. When he finally came over, I indicated my displeasure at having had to wait so long. Rather than apologize, he returned my snarky attitude with a snarky attitude of his own, and from then on, an uncomfortable feeling hung between us with every interaction.

The whole encounter cast an unpleasant pall on the evening. But what most preoccupied me was knowing that I'd started it all. I'd arrived at the restaurant in a testy mood, and in my preoccupation, I hadn't considered that a busy restaurant meant a busy bartender. Rather than realizing he was simply too busy to notice me, I made it personal: *he was ignoring me.* Trapped in my own small world, I had taken offense, and I felt bad about it.

After thinking the situation through, I got the bartender's attention and apologized for my behavior. He was surprised — probably because we humans don't apologize to each other that much when it means admitting fault — and also pleased. His attitude toward me shifted instantly. He was warm, friendly, and attentive the rest of the evening, and he even comped us two beers.

My apology made the evening a much more enjoyable experience for all of us. But afterward, I found something more to take away from the encounter.

What struck me was that the conflict, while initially disruptive and unpleasant, had actually created the opportunity for a deeper, stronger relationship to emerge. Had the conflict not occurred, we would have been to him just one more forgettable customer, and he would have been to us just one more forgettable service person.

But the conflict changed all that. Yes, we'd torn the fabric of our admittedly thin relationship. But once I'd managed to calm down, consider my part in the conflict, and apologize, the fabric was not just mended, it had gotten *stronger*. Interpersonal integration had cultivated neural integration — for both of us. We each became friendlier. We interacted more. He became more attentive, responsive and generous — and he comped us two beers! We left a big tip!

This experience affirms for me the value of prioritizing relationship over being right. Had I justified my behavior and held on to feeling slighted, leaving just my lower brain in charge, each of us would have left the encounter with our neural integration a little weaker, a little more frayed, and feeling more bad than good.

Understand the Other's Story

PBS and AAA(A) are all useful strategies to help get a relationship back on an even keel, allowing us to calmly and creatively re-engage in the conversation. But there's one more strategy for reconnecting a fractured relationship that I believe is the most effective of all: *understand the other's story*. Because behind every belief, every action, there's a story that, if we knew it, would transform our judgment and condemnation into understanding and compassion.

That's a big claim, so let me share an experience that helps illustrate what I'm talking about.

> *My son was in middle school, going through a program to earn his black belt in karate. Everyone in the program was near his age, except for one man in his early 40s.*
>
> *I watched this man practice and quickly noticed how seriously he took his training. Too seriously, I thought. His level of fervor and concentration exceeded the bounds of what seemed normal for a man his age, and I found myself judging him. There's something off about this guy, I thought. He needs to relax, chill out and gain a little perspective. He seemed nice enough, but when I considered becoming friends with him, I felt this behavior was a deal breaker.*
>
> *Later I learned more about him and discovered he'd actually enrolled in the program with his young daughter. They'd made a commitment to get their*

black belts together, knowing that they'd share an experience they'd always treasure. But a few months into the program, his wife and daughter were in a serious car accident and his daughter was killed.

That piece of information clarified everything for me. The intensity he brought to his training wasn't about the black belt. It was about his daughter and his grief. It was about honoring her memory by finishing alone what they'd started together. It was about keeping his daughter with him a little longer as he struggled to come to terms with his loss.

As you might imagine, once I learned his larger story, all my judgment vanished. I was propelled out of my story and into his — a story of deep pain and suffering.

Learning the reality of that man's life punctured my inflated sense of self — the attitude that had caused me to judge him harshly — and allowed me to regain my own humility and humanity.

So, here's the proposition I'd like you to consider: *at the heart of every conflict is an unspoken story* — a story that, once known, reveals the deep humanity of "the other" and transforms our judgment, hurt, or anger into understanding and compassion.

It may take a while to find it, to get beyond the "surface" story to the one that has this transformative power. But we'll know we've found it when what we hear is not just "their" story but also *our* story — the story we can all relate to by virtue of being human. That's where we find true common ground. That's where we find the relationship that can never stay broken for long.

Of course, finding that story doesn't necessarily mean the conflict goes away — although it might. What it *does* mean is that our attitude toward the person with whom we're having the conflict is no longer poisoned by our negative emotions and harsh judgments. This gives us the opportunity to engage with greater understanding and empathy, allowing us to repair the relationship and move forward in the dialogue.

Experiencing the Power of Story

So how do we test the validity of this reconnecting strategy? What does it look like in a difficult conversation? Let me start by sharing how I integrate it into my workshop.

The process I use is simple, an adaptation of an exercise called Peaks and Valleys. People have 10 minutes to write or draw their life story — from birth to present — on a piece of paper (actually a piece of transparency paper, for reasons that become clear later in the book). Their story should include 7-10 key events that represent the high and low points of their lives — their peaks and valleys — and how each of those events helped shape their values, attitudes, and beliefs.

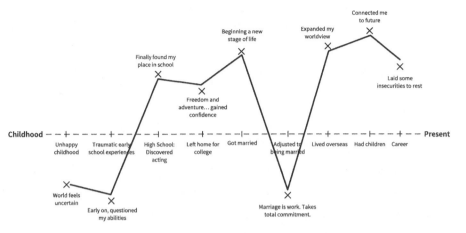

Example of a completed Peaks and Valleys life story exercise.

Then they pair with someone they don't know, or at least don't know well. Each gets 10 minutes to share their story, during which their partner *only listens*. No comments or questions! Once the person finishes their story, their partner has five minutes to ask questions that clarify or explore something the person said. When those five minutes are up, the two people switch roles.

When the storytelling is finished, I ask a few of the pairs to share their experience. Many express being moved to tears because no one has ever before given them the gift of such deep listening. Others share the surprise and joy of being able to connect so closely with someone who, minutes before, was a complete stranger.

There's something powerful about letting down our

The Resonance Circuit

You might be wondering what makes stories so powerful. Once again research in neuroscience helps shed some light. Stories, it turns out, *bring brains together* — especially stories that elicit authentic and intimate emotional connection.

While people the world over may have different ideas, values, and beliefs, feelings are universal.[1] And positive feelings in particular provide a powerful pathway to connect across our differences. Neuroscientists call this pathway our "resonance circuit."

At the heart of our resonance circuit is a group of neurons science has only recently discovered, called *mirror neurons*. Tucked inside our limbic system, these neurons have a special property that allows us to "mirror" or "simulate" the internal emotional state of others. In other words, they let us feel "a state similar" to that of another person.[2]

It's a phenomenon we've all experienced. When we see someone get hurt, we wince. When we see a mother mourning over the loss of a child, we tear up. When we see someone laugh and smile, we almost invariably laugh and smile ourselves. These are our mirror neurons at work.

When we simulate the internal state of another, we feel

compassion and empathy, allowing us to become linked together "as a part of a resonating whole," according to neuro-psychiatrist Daniel J. Siegel. There's also evidence that this kind of "resonance" accelerates the formation of relationships, enables large-scale cooperation, and, as noted earlier, stimulates "the neural circuitry responsible for giving meaning, responding flexibly, and shaping the subjective experience of an emotionally vibrant life."[3]

---

1   For more on this idea, see "Cross-Cultural Recognition of Basic Emotions Through Nonverbal Emotional Vocalizations," by Disa A. Sauter, Frank Eisner, Paul Ekman, and Sophie K. Scott, *Proceedings of the National Academy of Sciences of the United States of America* 107, no.6 (Feb 9, 2010): 2408-2412, doi:10.1073/pnas.0908239106.
2   Siegel, *The Developing Mind*, 157.
3   Ibid., 169.

guard, being vulnerable and sharing our humanity with another. It's a way to untie the Gordian knot of self-preoccupation and self-doubt, freeing us to experience the joy of acceptance and connection, as we discover we're not that different.

And perhaps most important of all, sharing our stories can bridge those seemingly unbridgeable differences. Here's one example from Amy, a workshop participant who shared this story with me by email:

When an older gentleman with a "Trump Tower" notebook sat down next to me at the training, I took a deep breath and just prayed that the workshop would give me some tools to manage whatever interactions might transpire with this guy.

Later, he ended up being my partner for the 'life story' sharing exercise, and we developed quite a connection.

I'm married to a combat veteran, and that has flavored my life (good, bad and ugly) for the past 12 years. It turned out that the man with the Trump Tower notebook was a Vietnam veteran who has dealt with many of the same struggles and was able to empathize in a way that only a veteran or family member can and to offer the benefit of wisdom that only comes with age.

So, this was quite a slap in the face for me to realize the value of letting go of our snap judgments.

*Had I not been forced to do so, I never would have
pursued a conversation or developed a connection
with this man.*

Amy's story helps illustrate that what we typically think
of as common ground —shared opinions, attitudes, and
beliefs — is in reality a false floor. Beneath it is something
far more stable and encompassing: the common ground of
universal and deeply felt human experience.

Getting the Story: The Art of Asking Questions

At this point you might be thinking, *that's all well and good
for a workshop where you have a lot of control over the environment, but most difficult conversations don't happen that way.
They're more organic, arising unexpectedly, like the two women
who met at the abortion rally. Can you imagine them breaking out pen and paper and launching into a Peaks and Valleys
storytelling exercise? Doubt it!*

Well, hold on. What if one of the women had the presence of mind to pause the conversation, acknowledge that
the current environment was hardly conducive to a productive dialogue, and suggested meeting later at a more quiet
and neutral location? Perhaps then the other woman (who
perhaps read this book!) might have said, "You know, I
recently heard about a method that helps people bridge
their differences — a storytelling exercise. Would you be
willing to try it as part of our dialogue?"

The Power of Resolution

A common question I get at this point in the workshop is "Why should I bother to seek resolution with a person whose views or actions I find hurtful or reprehensible?" One reason, particularly true today, is because those tend to be the people with whom we most need to find common ground so that we can work together to address our many challenges. Another reason, which we just discussed, is because to do so allows us to become more deeply integrated, which in turn makes us feel more alive, more energetic, more "whole."

In other words: resolution feels really, really good. A quick story:

> Early in my career I had a boss, Jack, who was a terrible micromanager. I hated working for him, and wanted nothing more than to see him get fired so that I'd be free to do as I pleased, without having to explain or justify my actions.
>
> And what was it like for Jack to have me as an employee? I drove him crazy. He felt my resistance at every turn, and the more I resisted, the more he felt the need to micromanage.
>
> It was an untenable situation. Every meeting was filled

with tension and animosity. I doubted I could stay in the job much longer, and he probably doubted he could have me as an employee much longer, too.

And then one day, the proverbial poop hit the fan. We were in a meeting together, just the two of us, and I blew up. (I flipped my lid!) I vented all my frustration at working with him, expressing in no uncertain terms how demotivating and frustrating it was to always be questioned and second-guessed.

His response? He blew up at me, telling me what a pain in the butt I was to work with, and —mirroring my own comments about him — how frustrating it was to always be questioned and second-guessed. (How often we reflect each other in that way!)

But once the explosion was over, something surprising happened. I didn't quit, and he didn't fire me. Instead, through some mysterious healing alchemy, the air was cleared, our mutual brains were reconnected, and we looked at each other and smiled. Somehow, we not only understood each other better, we liked each other better, too.[1]

I thanked him. He stood up, reached across his desk, shook my hand with enthusiasm and said, "Thank *you*."

From then on, we were not only good friends and a great team, but also, for the next several years, a special ritual would take place at the company's annual holiday party: Jack would get drunk, come over to where I was standing, throw his arm around me and recount the whole episode. Then he'd look me in the eye and with deep feeling tell me it was the best experience of his life. I knew he meant it, and I suspected it might have been the first time he'd ever known what true resolution felt like.

It *does* feel incredibly good to resolve issues in a relationship, and now we know, at least in part, why. We experience more aliveness because in a sense, we *are* more alive: we have more of our brain working for us, we have more of our energy creatively directed, and we experience more joy in our relationships.

1   We never know exactly how resolution in a relationship will occur, but blowing up at your boss is probably not a strategy I'd ever recommend: I was young and ignorant and lucky things turned out the way they did. The only point I'm making is that when we resolve a conflicted or broken relationship, the rewards can be immense.

Who knows? It might have led to a very different outcome.

But let's say, for whatever reason, you're in a situation where that isn't an option. The conversation is happening here and now, and you have to deal with it. What do you do? How you take it to a deeper level?

Here's a simple suggestion: Set aside your agenda (prioritize the relationship!), and as Megan Phelps-Roper recommends, *ask good questions* — questions that get to the story *behind* the story, the one that explains why the other person thinks or believes the way they do.

Let's continue using the abortion conversation from Chapter 1 as an example. I'd mentioned that the first woman to speak began by telling a story that helped explain why she was pro-life. Here's a little more about what she said:

I had a friend who was pregnant. She's what you'd consider a low-income crisis pregnancy . . . and so I decided that I was going to step up — and this was years and years ago, before I ever became a pro-life advocate — and I told her, I said, 'Look, I feel so bad for you, I feel so sorry for you. I'm doing well, I'll pay for everything, I'll take care of the baby, I'll adopt the baby.'

And she went to Planned Parenthood, and they talked to her right then and there, talked her into having an abortion! Even if you're dirt poor, there are so many services, there are so many resources. I opened my home! I mean, how many of these people have done that?

The second person, if you'll recall, acknowledges the story, but doesn't follow up. Instead she launches into her own talking points, missing an opportunity to learn the deeper story behind this woman's extraordinary offer to pay for everything and even adopt the baby. That's not something most of us would do! And it's a clear signal there's some meaningful story in her life that motivates her values and choices.

Simply asking the question *why* can help reveal that story. What if the second woman had said, "That's pretty amazing! Why did you make that offer? Is there something you've experienced that made this so important to you?" Maybe she'd have discovered that the first woman was never able to get pregnant, or perhaps had lost a child, leaving a void she longed to fill. Or that she had been searching for more meaning and purpose in her life, and what better purpose (in her view) than to save an un-born baby?

That it was likely none of these is not the point. The point is that there's *some* story that helps explain the woman's beliefs and actions. And once revealed, it would have created an opportunity for the second woman to go deeper — to express empathy as well as interest in learning more — to tease out the finer details that, when uncovered, might surprise and enlighten them both.

In short, she could have given the other woman the gift of her total attention, the gift of just listening. Odds are, like the many people in my workshop, it would have been the first time the first woman had ever received such a gift.

Imagine the relationship that might have emerged after that conversation, and how it could have placed their disagreement over abortion in a broader and less volatile context — just as Amy's conversation with the Vietnam War vet made the man's possession of a Trump Tower notebook loom far less large in her mind. Instead of a trigger for her amygdala, it became one artifact in the life of a valuable and multi-dimensional human being.

In both cases, having now connected at a deeper level, it's not hard to imagine a conversation not just about Trump, or about abortion, but more importantly, about our country, our vision of the future, and where our visions overlap so we can begin working together.

Beyond Values and Beliefs

Earlier I posed the proposition that *at the heart of every conflict is an unspoken story.* My experiences leading my workshop have led me to add a corollary to that proposition: *relationships rooted in our common humanity cannot be uprooted by differences in values and beliefs.*

Let me unpack that a little.

It's common and normal for our closest relationships to be with people who share our cherished values and beliefs. To use Daniel J. Siegel's language, with those people we have a deep level of *interpersonal integration.*

It's also, unfortunately, common to believe that we can *only* be close to people who share our cherished values and beliefs. This assumption leads to widespread interpersonal *dis-integration*, dividing families, communities, states, our nation and even the world at large — moving us closer, as author Alan Jacobs says, "to that primitive state that the political philosopher Thomas Hobbes called 'the war of every man against every man.'"[4]

As we've seen, however, when interpersonal integration occurs at the level of our common humanity — when we're able to recognize ourselves in others, even those we think of as "the enemy" — the relationships we build around that common human bond supersede differences in values and beliefs, giving us a solid foundation to better understand, resolve or even synthesize our disparate perspectives.

REFLECT

Have you ever fully resolved a torn relationship — one in which there used to be tension or ill will, and together you were able to turn it around?

If so, try to remember how it felt — how it impacted your spirit, your energy, your attitude. Take a few moments to write about the experience. If you're going through this book with others, share your reflections.

If you haven't had such an experience, use this as an opportunity to reflect on why not.

Personal Assessment #2

Think again about the difficult conversation you wrote about in Chapter 1.

Is there something in your story that, if shared, would help move it toward resolution?

Assume there's something in the other person's story that — if you knew —would help move the conflict toward resolution. How might you find out? Will you?

1   Dirk Jan Ardesch, Lianne H. Scholtens, Longchuan Li, Todd M. Preuss, James K. Rilling, and Martijn P. van den Heuvel, "Evolutionary Expansion of Connectivity Between Multimodal Association Areas in the Human Brain Compared with Chimpanzees," *Proceedings of the National Academy of Sciences of the United States of America* 116, no.14 (Apr 2, 2019): 7101–7106, doi:10.1073/pnas.1818512116.
2   George Vaillant, *Spiritual Evolution: A Scientific Defense of Faith* (New York: Potter/TenSpeed/Harmony, 2008), 36.
3   Daniel J. Siegel, *The Developing Mind: How Relationships and the Brain Interact to Shape Who We Are*, 2nd ed. (New York: Guilford Publications, 2012), 169.
4   Jacobs, *How to Think: A Survival Guide for a World at Odds*, 27.

New Survival Strategy #2:

See Beyond Your Story, Part 1

Could it be there is another ground on
which to plant our feet?

— Michael Pollan, *How to Change Your Mind*

T he first new survival strategy — *prioritize the rela-*
tionship over being right — becomes much easier when
practiced with the second strategy: *see beyond your story.*

Think back to Megan's TED talk, and how David was
able to stay in relationship with Megan despite her hateful and intolerant views. One reason he was able to do
so was because he separated Megan's *story* — the values,
attitudes, and beliefs she was inculcated with from birth
— from Megan's *humanity.* He knew that underneath her
hate and intolerance was a human being he could connect
with. As Megan shared in her TED talk, "We'd started to

see each other as human beings, and it changed the way we spoke to one another."

More important, perhaps, is that David was also able to separate from his *own* story — to see it within the context of a larger *sense of self*, one not so easily threatened or triggered by the harmful views of another.

The outcome of David's approach is worth revisiting: by seeing beyond both his own and Megan's story, David created the opportunity for Megan to do likewise. In particular, it allowed her to see her past not as something she was irreversibly locked into, but something she could step back from and re-examine. She could then make new choices based on new information and experiences.

Clearly, this ability to see beyond our story — freeing ourselves from the triggers that activate our primitive survival drive in unproductive and unhealthy ways — unleashes extraordinary possibilities for change. Understanding and accessing this power is the purpose of our second new survival strategy.

Beyond Our Story

Seeing beyond our story so that we don't get triggered by the threatening views of another isn't easy. As we learned, our lower brain is unable to parse the difference between a threatening bear and a threatening belief — and responds to both with the same limited set of responses: fight, flee, or freeze.

But knowing *what* triggers our survival drive doesn't tell us *why* that trigger is so powerful. After all, not every idea, belief, or opinion that runs counter to our own triggers our fight/flee/freeze reaction. And those that trigger mine don't necessarily trigger yours.

So, what's going on? Why do certain ideas, beliefs, and opinions rise to the level of an imminent, life-ending threat, and others don't?

It's an essential question. To answer it, we need to look more deeply into our own story: how it informs—and often constricts—our sense of self.

Our Story, Our Self

Our "story" is the sum of our life experiences, from birth to the present moment. Among the major factors shaping our story are our family; our race, ethnicity and gender; our religious upbringing (or the absence thereof); our physical or emotional traumas; and of course, the dominant culture of the society in which we live.

While psychologists have long known that past experiences play a profound role in determining our sense of self, only recently have we understood why: experiences, neurologists tell us, actually *shape how our brain is structured*, creating powerful mental models through which we see, understand, and interact with the world.

Author Michael Pollan offers a useful metaphor to help us understand how this brain sculpting process works.

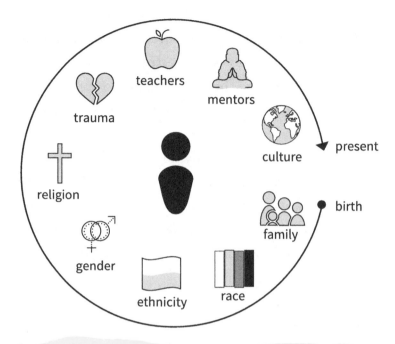

Our "story" is the sum of our life experiences from birth to the present moment.

Imagine sleds gliding down a hill covered in snow, carving out well-marked trails in their path. In Pollan's metaphor, the fresh snow represents our brain, the sleds represent our experiences, and the resulting trails are the neural pathways left in their wake — distinct patterns of synaptic connections responsible for such processes as memory, emotion, and self-awareness.[1]

In other words, our experiences create the neural networks out of which our sense of self arises.

Moreover, there's a *particular* neural network associated with our sense of self. It's called the Default Mode

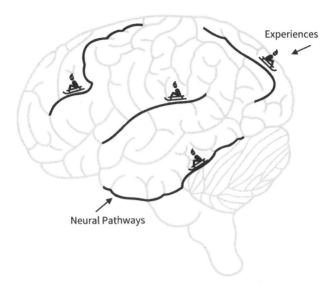

Experiences

Neural Pathways

Like sleds carving pathways on a snowy hill, our experiences carve the neural pathways that shape how our brain is structured.

Network (DMN) — "default mode" because it's active when we're at rest. It's the place "where our minds go to wander—to daydream, ruminate, travel in time, reflect on ourselves, and worry."[2]

Because it's associated with our sense of self, the DMN is sometimes called the "me network." I call it the "story-self."

Whatever you call it, the important point is that our sense of self has a clear neurological basis, which begins to explain why we so deeply identify with our story, and why we're willing to go to such lengths to protect and defend it.

It also helps explain why we *shouldn't* go to such lengths to protect and defend our story.

"Neurons That Fire Together, Wire Together"

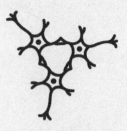

The patterning of our brain through experience is explained by something called Hebb's Rule, first postulated by neuropsychologist Donald Hebb, which can be summarized as "neurons that fire together, wire together." When we have traumatic or repetitive experiences, or repetitive thoughts, the corresponding neural patterns strengthen and can eventually take on a life of their own. This is why learning to ride a bike or learning to play an instrument become nearly automatic; why certain thoughts or feelings can become obsessive; and why certain emotions from the past can be easily triggered in the present.

The Limits of Our Story

Why should we be less protective of our story-self? To begin to answer that question, think back to the exercise in Chapter 3 where people were invited to write or draw their life story on a transparency sheet. Imagine you've done that exercise and that your once-clear sheet is now filled with words and images that reflect the peaks and valleys of your life.

Now imagine holding the sheet up to your face and looking through it.

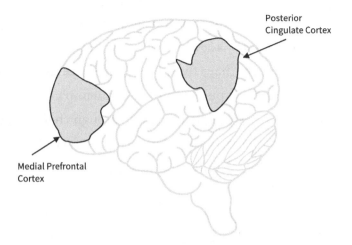

Posterior Cingulate Cortex

Medial Prefrontal Cortex

The Default Mode Network, sometimes called the "me network," is a group of interconnected brain regions associated with our sense of self. The main regions are the medial prefrontal cortex (mPFC) and the posterior cingulate cortex (PCC).

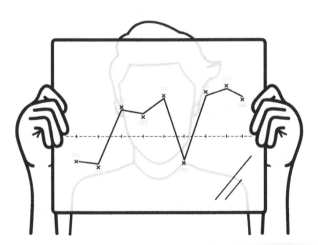

Our story creates a filter through which we see, interpret, and interact with the world.

How clearly are you able to see?

When I do this demonstration in my workshop, the room is filled with laughter and murmurs of insight as people confront, perhaps for the first time, how their story-self obstructs their perception. The murmurs of insight continue when people, still looking through their sheets, look at one another and see the how the obstruction — and the potential for misunderstanding and miscommunication — doubles.

In my workshop, I use this demonstration to highlight four crucial limits of our story-self:

1. Our story-self sees the present through the lens of the past.

As we've seen, experiences shape how our brain is structured, creating mental models through which we interpret the world. This means we're never quite looking at things as they are. As neuropsychiatrist Daniel J. Siegel puts it:

> *Each of us filters our interactions with others through the lenses of mental models created from patterns of experiences in the past.*[3]

This, as you can imagine, has important implications. Think back to our metaphor of sleds gliding down a hill, carving out deep trails in the snow. Future sleds, following the path of least resistance, will gravitate toward those same trails. Similarly, new experiences, following the path of least resistance, will tend to fall into preexisting *neural* pathways, as our brain looks for a match with some past event — a handy evolutionary shortcut to help us quickly make sense of our world: *if current event A looks like past event B, here's what it means and what we need to do.*

Often that's a good thing. It's why we only need to learn *once* not to put our hand on a hot stove. But it's not *always* a good thing. Sometimes we get it wrong and assume two events are similar when they're actually quite different. This brings us to the second limit of our story-self.

2. Our story-self can distort our perceptions and trigger our survival drive.

Distortions occur when present events get channeled along an existing neural pathway that's a poor match for what's really going on. For example, you see someone who you think is an old friend, but up close find he or she is a complete stranger.

Often the mismatch is harmless (if a bit embarrassing). However, it can lead to significant misunderstandings and overreactions. This is especially true when the chosen neural pathway is associated with a negative memory.

Let me give a short example. I grew up in a family

whose members were quick to blame and criticize, often unfairly. When such criticism was leveled at me, I was hurt. Later, as a married adult, I found that these forgotten hurt feelings brought some distorted perceptions into my marriage. When my wife would, on occasion, mistakenly accuse me of some mishap, feelings of injustice would well up in me, and I'd defend myself with an emotional fervor excessive to what the situation called for. (I "flipped my lid.")

"Memory," says Siegel, "is the way that past events affect future function."[4] In this situation, I channeled my wife's criticism along an old neural pathway associated with memories of harsh family criticism, activating an old emotional charge that sent hurt feelings from my childhood surging into the present — an unconscious form of payback for past grievances, but paid to someone who hadn't incurred the debt.

The key word in that last sentence is *unconscious*. I was unaware that my experiences growing up were the source material for my overreaction to my wife's criticism. Only when I recognized the connection between the past and my

WATCH

To learn more about how our brain constructs, and often distorts, our perceptions, check out this short, highly entertaining video by those brilliant folks at CrashCourse. Search YouTube for *Perceiving is Believing: Crash Course Psychology #7.*

overreaction was I able to formulate a more creative response to the present situation.

So if many of the distorting influences of our story-self are unconscious, how do we know when they have us in their grip? When we've exceeded what neuropsychiatrists call our "window of tolerance": the third limit of our story-self.

3. Our story-self creates — and limits — our "window of tolerance."

In your mind's eye, hold your transparency paper to your face once again and imagine your fingers grasping the edges of your paper. These edges form the outer boundaries of your window of tolerance: the zone within which you're able to function most effectively. As long as your interactions with the world stay within your window — as long as events reasonably align with your story-self's understanding of how things *should be* — you're able to maintain response flexibility: the ability to regulate your emotions and respond creatively.

Not so, however, with events or interactions *outside* your window of tolerance. These situations often present values, attitudes, and beliefs that challenge your understanding of who you think you are, or — often more important — who you think you need to be, triggering your fight/flee/freeze reaction. Siegel describes it this way:

In states of mind beyond the "window of tolerance," the pre-frontally mediated capacity for response flexibility is temporarily shut down. The "higher mode" of integrative processing has been replaced by a "lower mode" of reflexive responding.[5]

Being unjustly criticized or blamed by my wife was outside my window of tolerance. It activated old and — most importantly — *unconscious* hurt feelings, and my instinctual reaction was to aggressively fend off

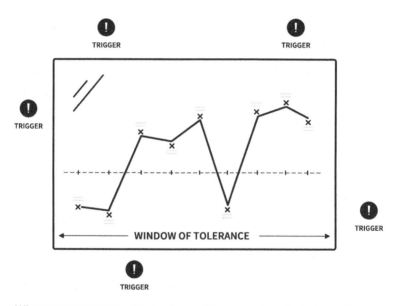

When events or experiences in our life exceed our "window of tolerance," they can trigger our survival drive and reduce our response flexibility.

REFLECT

Draw your "window of tolerance" using as a model the illustration below. Think about what lies outside your window. What attitudes? What behaviors? What beliefs? Write them down outside your window.

Reflect on how they got there. Are any of them connected in some way to your story? If you're reading this book with others, share your reflections.

WINDOW OF TOLERANCE

those feelings so that I could bring the situation *back* within my window.

Now you might be thinking *What's wrong with defending yourself against an unjust criticism? Isn't that what we all should do?* The answer is yes, but without the emotional baggage that can cause us to flip our lid and the situation to spin out of control. Think how much smoother things would have gone had I left my past in the past, and simply and calmly stated my innocence! Doing so could also have avoided a further complication: sometimes my aggressive efforts to get things back within *my* window of tolerance would push my wife outside *hers*, setting the stage for a spiraling, all-out argument increasingly disconnected from the original trigger.

There's a (conceptually) simple solution to all this, of course, and that's to *expand* our window of tolerance so that certain events, ideas, and beliefs no longer trigger our fight/flee/freeze reaction. This enlarged zone within which we can be present and responsive allows us to be more open, creative, resilient, and resourceful in a greater range of circumstances.

There's just one problem, and we know it well: expanding our window of tolerance means opening ourselves to points of view counter to our beliefs and values which, as we've seen, can feel like an existential threat to our story-self. Rather than expand our window, our first impulse, as my story illustrates, is to try to preserve it — a walled perimeter that keeps threats to our story-self at bay.

This leaves us in a kind of "conversational catch-22." To keep from flipping our lid when our story-self is threatened, we need to expand our window of tolerance. But we refuse to expand our window of tolerance when it threatens our story-self!

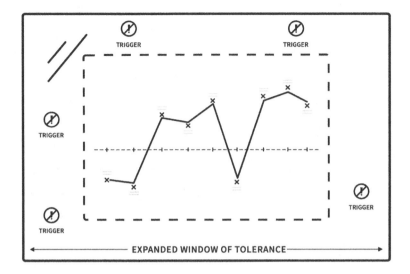

Expanding our window of tolerance enlarges the zone — and the circumstances — within which we can be present and responsive, allowing us to be more open, creative, resilient, and resourceful.

The situation now feels more tangled than ever. Is there any way to untangle it? Yes, and the key is in understanding the fourth and final limit to our story-self.

4. Our story-self thinks it's our "whole self."

Our story-self is so ingrained at the neural level that we tend to believe it's the entirety of who we are. That's why threats to our story-self exceed our window of tolerance and trigger our ancient survival drive. We indeed feel our very existence is on the line. No "story," no "self."

In a podcast on the neuroscience of changing your mind, a neuroscientist at the University of Southern

Expanding Our Window of Tolerance: Implicit vs. Explicit Memories

To better grasp how our story-self shapes and often distorts our present perceptions — and limits our window of tolerance — it's helpful to understand the difference between *explicit* and *implicit* memories.

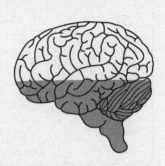

Explicit memories — triggered by, say, a familiar smell or piece of music — arrive with an internal awareness that we're recalling something from the past.

When *implicit* memories are triggered, however, there's no sense of recalling anything at all. Forgotten, buried under painful traumas, or encoded in early childhood before our brain is able to form explicit memories, *implicit* memories act as unconscious "mental models" — invisible filters through which we interpret and react to the present moment.

In neuropsychiatrist Daniel J. Siegel's words, implicit memories have the power to "influence our conscious experience without our knowing that something from the past is having an impact on our lives."[1]

Since we don't have a conscious sense of *having* an implicit memory, how then do we know when we're under its influence?

One way, as we've discussed, is when we exceed our window of tolerance and fall under the spell of strong, uncontrolled, negative emotional reactions — like flipping our lid.

In the story I shared, my early childhood experience of being unjustly criticized was an implicit memory at work. And because it was a *painful* implicit memory, when reactivated by my wife's criticism, it manifested as an unconscious wave of negative emotions and behaviors that were clearly counterproductive.

So when this happens to us, what can we do? How do we expand our window of tolerance so that we're no longer in the grip of our fight/flee/freeze reaction?

The first step, according to neuroscientist Alex Korb, is to become aware of and *name* the emotions that have us in their grasp. Doing so engages our ventrolateral prefrontal cortex, "which then communicates through the medial prefrontal cortex to reduce amygdala reactivity."[2] Korb describes it in simple terms:

> *Putting emotions into words—however hokey that sounds—actually rewires your brain circuits and makes you feel better.*[3]

Once we're in a calmer state, we can take the second step of what Siegel calls "memory integration": reconnecting our "implicit" memory to its "explicit counterpart," expanding our window of tolerance and giving us more conscious control over our reactions.

Once I made the connection between my emotional reaction to my wife's criticism and the relevant memories of my childhood, my implicit memory integrated with my explicit memory, giving me greater understanding of what exactly had me in its grip. Now integrated into my conscious awareness, that particular memory can no longer cause havoc.

Today, when a similar situation arises, I may still feel the cold shadow of the old implicit memory, but the emotions are far less intense, and I retain the ability to choose a more constructive and creative response.

1   Daniel J. Siegel, *The Developing Mind: How Relationships and the Brain Interact to Shape Who We Are*, 2nd ed. (New York: Guilford Publications, 2012), 383..
2   Alex Korb, *The Upward Spiral: Using Neuroscience to Reverse the Course of Depression, One Small Change at a Time* (New Harbinger Publications, 2015), 134.
3   Ibid., 46.

California uses an analogy to help explain this dynamic. He compares the way our brain constructs our story-self to the way we construct a house.[6] In a house, everything is connected to everything else, and that's exactly how information is stored in our brain. So once a belief or value becomes part of our story-self, changing it might threaten the stability of the entire structure, especially if the belief or value is deeply held.

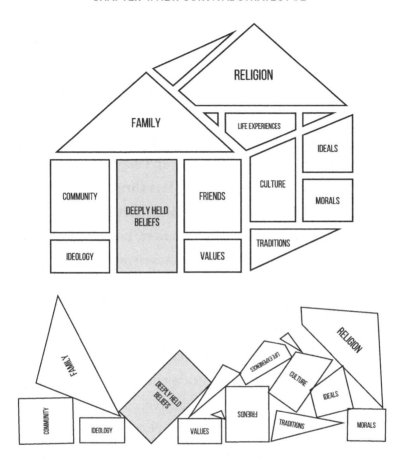

To our story-self, a deeply held belief is like the loadbearing wall of a house — remove it and everything else collapses. This is one reason changing our beliefs can be so difficult.

In that case, changing our mind would be like removing one of our house's load-bearing walls, potentially causing the whole structure — our whole identity — to collapse.

Not an outcome toward which we typically gravitate!

Fortunately, studies in neuroscience and psychology offer us a much-expanded view of who we are. Far from being the whole house, our story-self is but one room in a veritable mansion. By consciously connecting with this much larger sense of self, we can more easily entertain other perspectives and expand our window of tolerance, thereby feeling less threatened.

So, what exactly is this larger sense of self? That's what we'll turn to next. But first, take some time to complete the third Personal Assessment.

Personal Assessment #3

Think again about your difficult conversation. Can you identify something outside your window of tolerance that's making the conversation difficult? If so, can you identify anything in your story that helps explain why it's outside your window of tolerance?

1   Michael Pollan, *How to Change Your Mind: What the New Science of Psychedelics Teaches Us About Consciousness, Dying, Addiction, Depression, and Transcendence* (New York: Penguin Press, 2018), 384.
2   Ibid., 302.
3   Daniel J. Siegel, *The Developing Mind: How Relationships and the Brain Interact to Shape Who We Are*, 2nd ed. (New York: Guilford Publications, 2012), 56.
4   Ibid., 46.
5   Ibid., 283.
6   The podcast, which I highly recommend, is called *You Are Not So Smart*. The specific episode I refer to is episode 93, "The Backfire Effect/Part 1."

⑤

New Survival Strategy #2:

See Beyond Your Story, Part II

In a series of experiments, psychologists Ethan Kross and Igor Grossmann of the University of Michigan, Ann Arbor, found that asking people to consider an emotionally charged issue as if they were a distant observer actually made people *wiser*.[1]

Specifically, they found that asking people to adopt an objective viewpoint about an issue they cared about deeply made them:

- more humble: they recognized the limits of their knowledge;
- more objective: they were less likely to get emotionally triggered;
- more open: they were more likely to listen and collaborate.

It's a fairly dramatic finding for such a simple instruction. So what's going on? Why would just *asking* people to be more objective yield such a significant shift in behavior?

One explanation has to do with the Default Mode Network (DMN), the part of our brain that lights up when we're thinking about ourselves. Not surprisingly, it does the opposite when we *forget* about ourselves, which the instruction in the experiment — think about the issue from a distanced perspective — was enough to do. Focusing our attention on a task, rather than on ourselves, disengages our DMN, quieting our story-self and allowing a different state of awareness to emerge — one with an apparently expanded set of qualities and capabilities. Because its main characteristic is a loss of "self"-consciousness, I call this expanded state of awareness our "unstory-self."

It's a state we've all experienced, though we may not have realized it. Think of something you love to do, something that totally absorbs your attention and causes you to lose all track of time. In those moments you're experiencing some variant of your unstory-self, or what psychologist Mihaly Csikszentmihalyi calls "flow." Common among people from all walks of life, flow has a consistent set of characteristics: our sense of self disappears, time speeds up or slows down, action and awareness merge (we become "one" with what we're doing), and our creativity and performance dramatically increase.

While the existence of the flow state has been recognized for decades, only recently have we understood its neurological basis. Two related findings in the field of neurobiology shed some light.

First, when we quiet our DMN, we deactivate our dorso-lateral prefrontal cortex (DLPFC), an area of the brain best known for self-monitoring. Steven Kotler, founder of the Flow Genome Project, puts it this way:

> *The DLPFC is our inner critic, that voice of doubt and disparagement. . . . With this area deactivated, we're far less critical and far more courageous, augmenting both our ability to imagine new possibilities and to share those possibilities with the world.*[2]

This release from self-monitoring also helps explain another recent finding: quieting our Default Mode Network makes us happier. In an influential paper titled "A Wandering Mind Is an Unhappy Mind," psychologists found that negative emotions — anger, fear, hurt, regret, sadness, anxiety — most strongly correlate with time spent in mind wandering, one of the main activities of the Default Mode Network (i.e., our story-self).

In contrast, positive emotions —love, joy, compassion, gratitude — are most strongly associated with a quiet Default Mode Network (i.e., our *unstory-self*). One reason: losing ourselves in an activity and silencing our inner critic appears to release a cocktail of feel-good neurotransmitters, such as dopamine, endorphins, and serotonin.

But it's not just about feeling good. These neurotransmitters also enhance creativity and performance, unleashing what Kotler calls "the three horsemen of rapid-fire problem-solving."

- We become more focused, "boosting imaginative possibilities by helping us gather more information."
- We're better at seeing the forest for the trees, "increasing our ability to link ideas together in new ways."
- We're better at "lateral thinking," the ability to solve problems by seeing them in a new and fresh light.

To sum up, our story-self — that familiar sense of self that arises out of our activated Default Mode Network — does not represent the totality of who we are: *there's another, more expansive "unstory-self" available to us.* It's one in which our inner critic ceases, negative emotions subside, and positive emotions rise in their place, broadening our window of tolerance. We become more flexible, more creative, and more open to new ideas — exactly the capacities we need to stay present and creative when dealing with difficult conversations.

So now that we know about the expanded capacities of our unstory-self, how do we access them?

Connecting with Our "Unstory-Self"

As we've seen, to connect with our unstory-self, we need

Intuition and the "Unstory-Self"

Waht is this new level of awareness associated with our unstory-self? Where does it come from?

One possibility is that it comes to us through our *intuition* — a more immediate and often non-linear state of ideation and "knowing" that's been credited with many scientific and artistic breakthroughs.

Steven Kotler observes that when we cultivate the qualities of flow (the qualities of our unstory-self), we trade "the fast-moving beta wave of normal waking consciousness" for "the far slower" waves that operate between alpha and theta waves: "that hypnogogic gap where ideas combine in truly radical ways."[1]

In other words, the flow state trades the slow, hard work of conscious processing for the "faster and more efficient processing of the subconscious" — the domain of our intuition.

Of course, both kinds of processing are needed. The reflective, analytical capacity of conscious processing keeps us grounded, while the creative problem-solving skills of flow help us break out of outmoded ways of thinking to discover new options and new possibilities.

1   Steven Kotler, "Flow States and Creativity," *Psychology Today*, Feb 25, 2014, https://www.psychologytoday.com/us/blog/the-playing-field/201402/flow-states-and-creativity/..

practices that quiet our Default Mode Network, freeing us from self-preoccupation, widening our window of tolerance, and releasing our creative and collaborative powers. In the course of this book, we've already introduced a few practices to help us do so. To recap:

- **PBS** (Pause, Breathe and Smile) and **AAA(A)** (Appreciate, Agree, Articulate, and Apologize) are all important steps that can help us back away from the cliff of "flipping our lid," opening the door to the expanded capacities of our unstory-self.
- **Sharing life stories** — particularly with someone we're in conflict with — takes the process further by creating the opportunity to connect at the level of our common humanity. Doing so helps us break free of the negative projections and judgments of our story-self and releases the empathy and compassion that naturally flow from our unstory-self.

Those are all important and powerful practices for connecting with our unstory-self, especially when we're in the midst of a difficult conversation. But we also need *daily* practices — exercises we engage in regularly to strengthen the neural connections associated with our unstory-self. If having a truly difficult conversation is like running a marathon, a daily practice is the training

Connecting with Our Unstory: The Power of Self-Acceptance

Sharing our personal stories not only helps us connect with others, it also helps us connect with ourselves.

When I facilitate the life story exercise in my workshop, the people who have the best experience report sharing more of their story than they'd planned. Usually this means that they surfaced certain life events that they'd normally have left hidden. So why would sharing so personally result in such a positive experience?

Just as we can be in conflict with others, we can also be in conflict with ourselves, pushing difficult-to-accept experiences and personality traits outside our window of tolerance, where they're unable to threaten our seemingly fragile story-self. But keeping these aspects of ourselves hidden is what keeps our Default Mode Network in business. Often, it's the things we don't like or accept about ourselves that we worry or feel guilty about, fueling our depressive self-preoccupation.

By sharing these parts of our self with another, we find they're not as threatening to our sense of self as we feared. By accepting them as part of our humanity, we've taken the wind out of their sails — wind that our unstory-self can now harness for more productive and joyful purposes.

we do beforehand so that we run the marathon well.

Following are four practices that are especially effective in strengthening our unstory-self's neural connections.

1. Meditating Mindfully

Research shows that mind-wandering — one of the principle activities of the Default Mode Network — takes up roughly 50 percent of our waking life and correlates with greater degrees of unhappiness.[3] That's a lot of time spent doing something that doesn't make us feel good. Worse, it's self-inflicted.

But here's the good news: one way to reduce the mind-wandering activity of the DMN is through mindfulness meditation: a practice of becoming aware of and then releasing self-referential thought so that we can stay focused on the present moment.

The scientific body of evidence on the benefits of mindfulness training probably exceeds that of any other practice we can mention. Just 10 minutes a day of mindfulness meditation has been found to reduce activity in our Default Mode Network (our story-self), while strengthening the functional connectivity among brain regions associated with our unstory-self. The benefits, by now familiar, include improved focus, improved cognitive flexibility, reduced affective reactivity (less likely to flip our lid), and "shifts away from a distorted or exaggerated view of oneself."[4]

Developing Our Observer

O
ne of the most important benefits of a mindfulness practice is developing the ability to observe our emotions from a distance, so that we're able to bring them under conscious control. We become a *witness* to our emotions, rather than feeling that we *are* our emotions.

What makes our "observer" capacity possible is the fact that "awareness and emotion are mediated by different regions of the brain."[1] This means we have the capacity to see that something's wrong without attaching emotion to the perception. A simple example: *2 + 2 = 5*. You can see it's wrong, but does it evoke any negative emotions? Odds are, no.

As we saw earlier, becoming aware of the emotions that have us in their grasp — developing our "observer" — engages our prefrontal cortex, "which then communicates through the medial prefrontal cortex to reduce amygdala reactivity."[2] Our emotions become less intense, more amenable to conscious control, and therefore less likely to launch an armada of unintended and unwanted consequences.

1   Alex Korb, *The Upward Spiral: Using Neuroscience to Reverse the Course of Depression, One Small Change at a Time* (Oakland, CA: New Harbinger Publications, 2015), 55.
2   Ibid., 134.

Three Common Mindfulness Practices

There are several different types of mindfulness meditation. Here's a quick introduction to the three most common forms:

- **Concentration Meditation:** A practice of focusing attention on the sensations of breathing. Helps to deactivate the DMN by shifting our attention away from self-related preoccupations (thinking about the past or future), and instead focusing on the present moment.

- **Loving-Kindness Meditation:** A practice of fostering positive feelings of love and care initially directed to a close loved one, and then to yourself, to others, and eventually to the whole world. Believed to foster acceptance of ourselves and others, and to increase concentration.

- **Choiceless Awareness Meditation:** A practice of observing our thoughts and feelings as they arise, labeling them—for instance, positive or negative, focused on self or others—but avoiding becoming absorbed in them.

There's also evidence that a meditation practice makes us smarter. It's been shown to stimulate the growth of neurons (gray matter)[5] and to strengthen the connectivity between neurons (white matter).[6] That's like increasing your computer's raw processing capabilities and then giving it more powerful programs to run.

Importantly, the benefits of mindfulness training also appear to be long lasting. Researchers at Yale University, studying the brains of experienced meditators, found the benefits of meditation — decreased activity in the DMN and increased connectivity among the brain structures "implicated in self-monitoring and cognitive control" — were present when the subjects were actively meditating *and* when they were simply in a resting state. This suggests, say the researchers, that "meditation practice may transform the resting-state experience into one that resembles a meditative state, and as such, is a more present-centered default mode."[7]

In other words, through meditation, we may be able to change the "default" state of our Default Mode Network, one where a tendency to mind-wander is replaced by a tendency to be present in the current moment.

2. Cultivating Awe

Dr. Loni Shiota, a behavioral scientist and pioneer in the study of awe and wonder, defines awe as an emotional response to extraordinary stimuli that "challenges our normal, day-to-day frame of reference" and is not yet "integrated into our understanding of the world."[8]

In other words, awe has the power to change our minds. It shakes up our internal landscape and launches us into new frontiers — inviting us to discover fresh ideas and new possibilities.

Not surprisingly, the experience of awe mirrors being in a state of flow. Caught up in the raptures of awe, we become "immersed in the present moment,

How Awe Sharpens Our Brain

Masters in the art of storytelling and persuasion know it's important to spark curiosity in the listener by creating a gap in their knowledge that they're then motivated to fill. The power of awe to change our minds, says behavioral scientist Michelle Lani Shiota, may come from that same dynamic. "So far, the clues suggest that awe's function may lie in how it makes us *think*. Awe involves a sense of uncertainty that we are compelled to try to resolve."[1]

1   Michelle Lani Shiota, "How Awe Sharpens our Brains," *Greater Good Magazine*, May 11, 2016. https://greatergood.berkeley.edu/article/item/how_awe_sharpens_our_brains/.

detached from our normal, mundane concerns." Our sense of self recedes, while at the same time we feel "connected with the world around us, in touch with something greater than ourselves."[9]

Awe, says Dr. Shiota, also disrupts the Default Mode Network's repetitive cycle of negative emotions, disengages our fight/flight/freeze responses, and reduces our "tendency to filter our current experience through what we think we already know." It increases humility, breaks down "us versus them" thinking, helps us "take in the bigger picture with greater discernment," and expands our understanding of self-interest.[10]

Words could not paint a more perfect portrait of our un-story self.

REFLECT

Experiences of awe can come from many sources, both physical and psychological. Examples include a beautiful landscape, a work of art, a moving speech or performance, an act of great altruism, or a spiritual or religious experience.

Think of an experience you've had that evoked the feeling of awe. Once you identify something, describe it in writing with as much detail as possible.

Afterward, consider the ways in which the experience might have altered how you see the world.

3. Practicing Gratitude

When it comes to unleashing the capacities of our un-story self, few practices are as immediately effective as cultivating gratitude. The subject of decades of research, gratitude has come to be known as "the mother of all virtues," and when you see its benefits, you'll know why.

Expressing gratitude, like experiencing awe, releases us from the negative preoccupations of our story-self, unleashing a bevy of feel-good neurotransmitters that stimulate feelings of joy, enthusiasm, love, happiness and optimism — all feelings associated with our unstory-self.

Grateful people also appear to have increased grey matter in their right inferior temporal cortex, an area of the brain associated with feeling rewarded when other people benefit. It's been shown to foster and strengthen relationships and increase feelings of generosity, kindness, appreciation, and a desire to be of service to others. It's also associated with being more cooperative, less selfish, and more forgiving. [11]

Expressions of gratitude don't just benefit the grateful. They can also spiral outward and motivate prosocial behavior in others. A Fordham University study found that simply thanking people for voting in the last election made them significantly more likely to vote in the next election than those who were just sent a postcard encouraging them to vote. The effect was consistent across a diverse range of voters.[12]

Another study looked at gratitude's role in maintaining romantic relationships. It found that those who felt appreciated by their partners also reported feeling more appreciation *for* their partners — translating into a higher level of commitment.[13]

The benefits of having a gratitude practice are not like Snapchat posts, disappearing in seconds. They last. One brain-scan study out of Indiana University found that following a gratitude letter-writing task, peoples' brains were still showing "significantly greater and lasting neural sensitivity to gratitude" even months later.[14] This suggests that our brain has something like a "gratitude circuit" and — following Hebb's Rule of "neurons that fire together, wire together" — that circuit can be strengthened over time. The more we practice gratitude, the less effort will be required to get us into a "gratitude zone." Eventually feelings of gratitude — and the associated benefits — may even become habitual.

4. Asking: How Am I Like You?

There's one last way I want to mention that can help you connect with your unstory-self the next time you're in a difficult conversation with someone whose actions, values, or beliefs lie outside your window of tolerance.

The Benefits of Gratitude:
A Quick Summary

A paper by the researchers at University of California at Berkeley's Greater Good Science Center summarizes the many benefits of cultivating gratitude.[1] According to the paper, gratitude:

- promotes humility;
- strengthens relationships;
- makes us more loving and forgiving;
- reduces stress and increases resilience to trauma;
- stimulates feelings of joy, enthusiasm, love, happiness, and optimism;
- reverses the harmful effects of negative emotions, restoring physiological and emotional balance;
- makes us more peaceful, less reactive and resistant;
- stimulates the growth of grey matter in the brain, improving our ability to process information;
- strengthens our heart;
- helps us recover more quickly from illness;
- promotes long-term thinking;
- helps us learn better;

- improves sleep, diet, and makes us more likely to exercise;
- encourages the development of other virtues such as patience, humility, and wisdom;
- inspires generosity, kindness, helpfulness, and inclusiveness;
- makes us more cooperative;
- generates more gratitude!

1   "The Science of Gratitude," a white paper prepared for the John Templeton Foundation by the Greater Good Science Center, University of California at Berkeley, https://www.templeton.org/wp-content/uploads/2018/05/Gratitude_whitepaper_fnl.pdf/.

Ask the question: "How am I like you?"

Be prepared: the answer can be immediately humbling, pulling the rug of self-righteous judgment right out from under your feet.

In my workshop, when I have people write down what's outside their window of tolerance, most common are things like arrogance, privilege, not listening, lying, greed, etc. These are attitudes and behaviors we all react to negatively, but none are strangers to us when we honestly consider our own thoughts and actions. Who among us has not been arrogant, rude, greedy?

Staying Grounded

I find it interesting that *humility* and *humanity* share the same root: *humus*, which means ground. To be humble, then, is to be grounded in our own humanity — aware of the truth of the Greek poet Terence's statement, "Because I am human, nothing human is alien to me."

Anytime we think we're better than someone else, we've become untethered from that ground — which may be why "being humbled" is often described as "being brought back down to earth."

Who has not failed to listen, or lied on occasion? Do we really have the right to condemn or harshly judge others who do the same?

I was thinking the other day about climate change, and about how many of us are incredulous that anyone could deny its reality. The evidence is so overwhelming that choosing to deny it is beyond our comprehension.

But is it? Go to the beach and you'll see hundreds of people — many of them, I'm sure, concerned about climate change — lying out to get a suntan, totally ignoring the science that says frying ourselves in the sun vastly increases the risk of skin cancer.

If you think about it, I'm sure you'll find examples of your own "inconvenient truths" — things you do that science has found run counter to your long-term health and well-being, but that you've either explained away as "well, you know, the findings aren't conclusive," or somehow convinced yourself you'll be the exception to the rule.

There's a quote by the ancient Greek poet Terence that's worth keeping in mind: "Because I am human, nothing human is alien to me." We are, after all, one human species — which means we all have the same capacities, the same human potential. It's only how and to what degree we manifest our potential that varies, based largely on the serendipitous circumstances of life experience.

It's disconcerting, of course, to see ourselves as a mirror image of the qualities and attributes we object to in others — but that's just our story-self at work. Our story-self is in part defined by what we believe separates us from others, but in the process it can separate us from our own humanity . . . casting pieces of ourselves out our window of tolerance.

By reintegrating these cast-out pieces, by seeing and accepting the fullness of our humanity, we're able to see and accept the humanity of "the other." Our attitude shifts from "me *versus* you" to "me *and* you." Now there's nothing to fight or flee from, and the powers of our unstory-self emerge as we engage the other with creativity, humility, and compassion.

We become, in other words, someone that "the other" might just be willing to listen to.

Personal Assessment #4:

Think again about your difficult conversation:
- List three things about the person or situation for which you're grateful.
- Does the list change your attitude or feelings toward the person or situation?
- If so, how?

1   Ethan Kross and Igor Grossmann, "Boosting Wisdom: Distance from the Self Enhances Wise Reasoning, Attitudes, and Behavior," *Journal of Experimental Psychology* 141, no. 1 (2012), 43–48.
2   Steven Kotler, *The Rise of Superman: Decoding the Science of Ultimate Human Performance* (London: Quercus Publishing, 2014), 50.
3   Matthew A. Killingsworth and Daniel T. Gilbert, "A Wandering Mind Is an Unhappy Mind," *Science* 330, no. 6006 (Nov 12, 2010), 932.
4   Judson A. Brewer, Patrick D. Worhunsky, Jeremy R. Gray, Yi-Yuan Tang, Jochen Weber, and Hedy Kober, "Meditation Experience Is Associated with Differences in Default Mode Network Activity and Connectivity," *Proceedings of the National Academy of Sciences of the United States of America* (PNAS) 108, no. 50 (December 13, 2011): 20254-20259, doi.org/10.1073/pnas.1112029108.
5   Britta K. Hölzelm, James Carmody, Mark Vangela, Christina Congleton, Sita M. Yerramsettia, Tim Gard, and Sara W. Lazara, "Mindfulness Practice Leads to Increases in Regional Brain Gray Matter Density," *Psychiatry Research: Neuroimaging* 191, no. 1 (January 30, 2011), 36-43.
6   Davide Laneri, Verena Schuster, Bruno Dietsche, Andreas Jansen, Ulrich Ott, and Jens Sommer, "Effects of Long-Term Mindfulness Meditation on Brain's White Matter Microstructure and its Aging," *Frontiers in Aging Neuroscience* 7, no. 254 (Jan 14, 2016), doi:10.3389/fnagi.2015.00254.
7   Meditation experience is associated with differences in Default Mode Network activity and connectivity. See Brewer et al., "Meditation Experience Is Associated with Differences in Default Mode Network Activity and Connectivity," doi.org/10.1073/pnas.1112029108.
8   Michelle Lani Shiota, "How Awe Transforms the Body and Mind," *Greater Good Magazine* video, 34.22. August 2016. https://greatergood.berkeley.edu/video/item/how_awe_transforms_the_body_and_mind/.
9   Ibid.
10   Lani Shiota, "How Awe Transforms the Body and Mind," https://greater-good.berkeley.edu/video/item/how_awe_transforms_the_body_and_mind/.
11   Glenn R. Fox, Jonas Kaplan, Hanna Damasio, and Antonio Damasio, "Neural Correlates of Gratitude," *Frontiers in Psychology* 6 (Sep 30, 2015): 1491, doi:10.3389/fpsyg.2015.01491.
12   Costas Panagopoulos, "Thank You for Voting: Gratitude Expression and Voter Mobilization," *The Journal of Politics* 73, no. 3 (Aug. 3, 2011), 707-717.
13   A.M. Gordon, E.A. Impett, A. Kogan, C. Oveis, and D. Keltner, "To Have and to Hold: Gratitude Promotes Relationship Maintenance in Intimate Bonds," *Journal of Personality and Social Psychology* 103, no. 2, 257–274.
14   Prathik Kini, Joel Wong, Sydney McInnis, Nicole Gabana, and Joshua W. Brown. "The Effects of Gratitude Expression on Neural Activity," *NeuroImage* 128 (2015), http://dx.doi.org/10.1016/j.neuroimage.2015.12.040.

6

New Survival Strategy #3:

Transform Resistance into Response

We delight in the beauty of the butterfly, but rarely admit the changes it has gone through to achieve that beauty.

— Maya Angelou, author and poet

Our third and last new survival strategy — *transform resistance into response* — is perhaps the most challenging to embrace — mostly because many believe that resisting the things we judge to be wrong is not just common sense, it's *noble and necessary*, a heroic standing-up for a greater good or higher virtue.

But let's look at resistance in a different light: as a powerful, yet often subtle manifestation of our ancient survival drive, which — when transformed into response — unleashes the power, creativity, and compassion of our highest human potential.

Think back one last time to Megan's story. Her Twitter friends no doubt felt resistance toward her views and actions, but they didn't let their resistance stand in the way of the relationship. They were able to move beyond it, to a place where they could respond to Megan, the *person*, not Megan, the *story*.

And as it turned out, it was by responding to Megan, the *person*, that Megan, the *story* was able to change.

Resistance: An Early Warning Signal

Resistance is an early warning signal that we're moving in the direction of neural dis-integration. Any time we're in resistance to *what is,* any time we're unable to respond

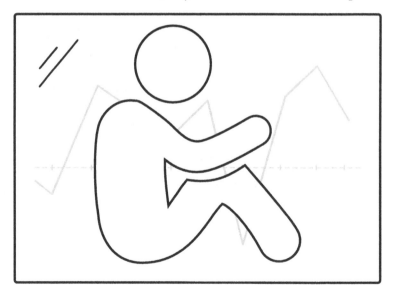

Resistance traps us in our story-self, cutting us off from the expanded perspective and creative capacities of our unstory-self.

creatively and compassionately to a given situation, we've exceeded our window of tolerance and are in some version of fight, flee, or freeze. We've weakened the neural connection to our pre-frontal cortex, blinded ourselves to the larger landscape of our common ground, and lost access to the full range of our creative capacities.

Metaphorically, I like to think of resistance as being stuck in my "story-self" — trapped inside a box of my own making, cut off from my "unstory" and the expanded perspective and creative capacities it provides.

To help illustrate just how dis-integrating resistance can be, let me share another personal story:

I was facilitating my Difficult Conversations workshop with a group of students in the living room of a cottage that was part of a large conference facility. Next to the living room was a small kitchen. We'd just begun a conversation about how to transform resistance into response when several conference interns noisily entered the cottage with trays of food that needed to be put into the kitchen refrigerator.

I was instantly annoyed, even angry, at this rude interruption, flummoxed by such a flagrant act of disrespect. I was, in other words, in a state of resistance. Worse, I was aware that as I sat there stewing, I was demonstrating my own inability to practice what I'd just been preaching: how to transform resistance into response!

It was a humbling experience, and after the interns left there was little choice but to do a mea culpa and use the episode as a learning opportunity for us all — a clear example of what happens when we get caught in resistance, caught in our story-self.

According to the perspective of my story-self, the interns' interruption was wrong — it shouldn't have happened. According the perspective of my wiser unstory-self, right or wrong, it was happening, and a creative response was possible. But the perceived egregious behavior was so outside my window of tolerance I couldn't see it. In the vernacular of our survival drive, I froze.

Only later, after I calmed down and reintegrated my upper and lower brain was I able to see the options hidden from me by my previously resistant state. One (now obvious) possibility: I could have suggested to the students that we pause our workshop and help the interns complete their task! That would have sped up the process, minimized the interruption, and, most importantly, effectively demonstrated what the workshop was all about.

Obviously, I missed the boat on that one. So, what then could I have done differently? Caught in resistance — stuck in my story-self — how could I have transformed it into response?

The Art of Surrender

As soon as I had consciously registered my resistance, I pretty much had only two choices: hold on to my resistance or surrender it. I chose to hold on, and we saw how that went. At other times, I've managed to surrender my resistance, and I can say from experience it's the far better option. Once we let go of our resistance, the barrier to our unstory-self dissolves, allowing us to see more creative and responsive pathways forward.

I realize this is not how people typically think about the word *surrender*. For many of us, *surrender* carries the connotation of waving the white flag and giving up our right to agency. But that's not what I'm advocating. Surrendering our resistance does *not* mean surrendering our goals or our right to take action. It *does* mean surrendering whatever stands in our way of taking effective and creative action — action that emerges from an expanded window of tolerance, free of the negative and often dehumanizing energies of an inappropriately triggered survival drive.

Now objectively, surrendering our resistance under those terms should be a slam-dunk. After all, who wouldn't want to be able to take effective, creative action? The answer, unfortunately, is *most of us*. Because once we're in the grip of resistance — a form of our powerful survival drive — breaking that grip can be extraordinarily difficult.

One way to make it easier, however, is to understand the relationship between our resistances and our attachments.

Attachment

Attachment, like surrender, has different connotations depending on the context. In early childhood development theory, having a strong emotional attachment to one's primary caregiver is thought to be critical for the child's physical and emotional health. In this sense, attachment is about *bonding* to another human being.

Another kind of attachment, and the way I'm using the word here, is *having an emotional investment in a particular outcome*, such that when that outcome is not realized, we get angry, or become obstinate, or sulk, or find ways to suppress or avoid our feelings of disappointment. In other words, we enter a state of resistance.

The connection between attachment and resistance highlights a subtle but important distinction: what triggers our resistance is not a particular outcome, but rather the *absence of the outcome we wanted*. It's an important distinction because it gives us agency over our resistance. Release the attachment, and the outcome ceases to be a trigger, leaving us free to respond in the most creative ways possible.

Take my example with the interns. I was attached — emotionally invested — in a workshop free of interruption. Had I been *detached* from the outcome, the interruption would never have triggered my resistance, and I could have more quickly discovered the range of creative responses available to me.

If this seems at all unclear or difficult to get your head around, it may be because we're strongly conditioned to believe that our resistance is a natural and justified reaction to some external event. In truth, our resistance simply reveals a pre-existing attachment to a certain reality prescribed — often unconsciously — by the mental models of our story-self and the boundaries of our window of tolerance.

This is one reason surrendering our resistance can be so difficult: it's based on an attachment unconsciously associated with the preservation of our story-self. To surrender our resistance and regain our full creative capacities, then, we need to become conscious of and release our attachments.

Identifying and Releasing Our Attachments

Usually we don't know we have an attachment until it trips us up and triggers our resistance. Once it does, however, we have an opportunity to bring the attachment to awareness so that it doesn't trip us up in the future.

While some attachments may be lightly held and easy to identify and release, others are more integral to our story-self, lying below our conscious awareness and serving as one of the load-bearing walls of our "identity house." In those cases, uncovering the source of our attachments can require more effort.

Detached, Not Disinterested

L ike the word *surrender*, the word *detachment* can be difficult for people. There's an assumption that letting go of our attachments means letting go of what motivates us: our passion, our convictions, our sense of purpose.

This, I believe, is a misconception that stems from looking at detachment only from the perspective of our story-self, rather than through the wider lens of our unstory-self.

Being emotionally attached to an outcome is inherently self-focused: an insistence that events unfold in a manner consistent with how *I* think things *should be*. In other words, my attachments reflect an attitude of "me first," my priorities over yours. And if I don't get my way, I'll be disruptive or withdraw from the relationship.

An attitude of detachment, on the other hand, is inherently *other focused*. It allows me to draw a larger circle and shift my attention from *me* to *we*, creating an attitude of openness and discovery. Rather than being focused on wanting my way at the expense of others, I'm focused on getting *our* way by *enlisting* others — a collaborative effort to find a solution that serves the well-being of everyone.

It could be that detachment, seen through the lens of our

story-self, looks devoid of life's energy because our story-self is not at the center. Instead, detachment puts our unstory-self at the center — the self that's able to be fully present, able to take in the bigger picture and the larger landscape of possibility.

Rather than dissolving our passion, convictions, and sense of purpose, detachment re-creates them in a larger, more inclusive context — *releasing* creativity rather stifling it, *eliciting* compassion and empathy rather than eliminating them.[1]

---

1   In fact, there's even evidence to suggest that detachment and empathy share a common neural circuit, one that involves the ventral and dorsal mid-prefrontal cortex and the amygdala. See "Augmenting Brain Function with Meditation: Can Detachment Coincide with Empathy?" by Shirley Telles, Nilkamal Singh, and Acharya Balkrishna, *Frontiers in Systems Neuroscience* (Oct 8, 2015), doi:10.3389/fnsys.2015.00141.

The Five Whys

One technique that can help us discover the source of our attachments is called the "Five Whys," a problem-solving strategy used in aviation safety to get to the root cause of an accident. The idea is that when asking why something happened, we need to look beyond the first, second, or even third answer in order to get to the true cause.

The best way to illustrate the Five Whys process, applied to an attachment, is through an example. Let me use — one last time — my story with the interns:

What outcome did you want?

I wanted people to not rudely interrupt my workshop.

1. Why?

Because it's inconsiderate.

2. Why does that matter?

Because they're acting like what I do doesn't matter.

3. Why does that bother you?

Because it's rude and inconsiderate!

4. Yes, you said that already. Why does it bother you to be treated as if you don't matter?

Well, to be honest, it hurts my feelings when people treat what I'm doing as unimportant.

5. Why does it hurt your feelings?

It's an old pattern of not feeling respected and valued, going back to my family upbringing . . . something I had not realized until now.

A few things to take away from this short example:

- By the third *why*, I got caught in a loop, basically repeating the answer I gave before. This is one reason we need to ask *why* several times — it helps us push through our unconscious defenses, the part of us that, for whatever reason, wants to keep our hidden parts hidden.

- When I finally got to the root of my attachment, it was far removed from "not wanting to be interrupted." It was to be thought well of so that I didn't have to deal with my underlying sense of insecurity. In other words, it was about the preservation of my story-self and staying within my window of tolerance.

- Finally, my attachment to the outcome (being *thought well of*) actually *undermined* that outcome. Had I not been attached, I could have, as mentioned, *modeled* the principles of my workshop, rather than just *talked* about them. (Wouldn't *that* have been impressive!)

So now that I've identified the source of my attachment,

where does this leave me? Recall the sidebar in Chapter 4, *Expanding Our Window of Tolerance: Implicit vs. Explicit Memories*. When we make unconscious emotional dynamics conscious (transferring them from implicit to explicit memory), we engage our prefrontal cortex, which in turn has a modulating effect on our amygdala's emotional reactivity. This means that, by itself, uncovering the root of our attachment is often enough to loosen its hold, allowing us to move past our resistance. (This, of course, may not be true when the root is tied to a particularly painful or traumatic memory. In that case, more personal work — and possibly professional help — may be required to weaken its emotional hold.)

The Five Whys can be a useful tool, especially when we're just starting out making the connection between past events and current behavior. Once we're well versed in our own story and how it has shaped us, however, the process can be more organic and faster.

Let me offer one other story to further illustrate this point:

Early in our marriage, my wife and I had the opportunity to travel throughout Southeast Asia, a part of the world where there's ample opportunity for bargaining. For my wife, because it was expected, bargaining was a given. For me, it was uncomfortable — something to be avoided.

Our different attitudes toward bargaining set

the stage for a number of arguments. When it came right down to it, my wife thought I was letting people take advantage of us; I thought she was creating negative encounters that strengthened the trope of the ugly American.

We'd reached a stalemate. She was attached to her way; I was attached to mine. For each of us, the other had become "the other" and the cause of the conflict.

At one point, I decided to reflect on why I was so attached to not bargaining. After all, it's a useful skill and an expected part of doing business in many parts of the world. What's more, done right, it's more likely to enhance a relationship than harm it.

My reflections took me back to my own story of growing up with an unpredictable, mercurial, and authoritarian father. Indirectness rather than confrontation was the best way to survive. I soon realized that this was the pattern at work for me when it came to bargaining. To me, the vendor was a threatening authority, and bargaining was too direct an approach. To get what I wanted, I fell back on my previously learned survival strategy: avoid (flee) confrontation.

I shared this insight with my wife, and it transformed our dynamic. Once I made the connection to my story, my resistance to bargaining lost its emotional intensity, and I began taking on more of the bargaining responsibilities. No longer the ground of warring ideologies, bargaining became a more pleasant experience for both of us — and also one we each could take or leave.

I hope these examples help make clear the role that our emotional attachments play in triggering our areas of resistance and making them difficult to surrender.

Letting Go of Control

One reason we resist threatening ideas or beliefs is because it gives us the illusion of control —  as if by resisting "the other," we might be able to change him or her. But as the cognitive neuroscientist Tali Sharot points out in her book *The Influential Mind: What the Brain Reveals About Our Power to Change Others*, surrendering our desire for control actually puts us in a *greater* position of influence, not less. When we let go of our desire to control, she says, we increase the other person's feeling of agency, a rewarding experience that calms their fear centers and makes them more receptive to what we have to say.

Understanding our areas of resistance and our attachments can guide us toward understanding our deeper, unconscious patterns, which — once exposed — greatly lose power.

To summarize this point: resistance is not "bad." Resistance is feedback, telling us there's something in our story that's been triggered, threatening our (limited) sense of self and preventing us from taking in the reality of what's in front of us. It's an indication that we need take a step back, reflect on our story, and uncover the specific source of the trigger. By doing so we can broaden our perspective, take in the views of "the other," and discover new ways to respond.

Surrendering Our Resistance: A Neurological Perspective

Another way to understand the dynamics of resistance, attachment, and surrender comes through the lens of neuroscience.

Recall that our experiences shape our brain, carving out neural pathways that generate the thoughts, feelings, and perceptions that give rise to our story-self. When we surrender our resistance — when we let go of our story-self's version of how things *should be* so that we can more clearly see them *as they are* — old and outdated neural patterns associated with our story-self begin to weaken, creating space for new patterns to emerge. In other words, when we surrender our resistance, we're literally *opening our mind* to new ways of seeing the world.

It's a miraculous process, made possible by a unique feature of the brain known as neuroplasticity: the brain's ability to grow new neurons and rewire itself in response to our changing experiences, circumstances, and thoughts.[1]

To our story-self, however, it's not so much miraculous as it is threatening. Our story-self wants to *preserve* its neural patterns, not eliminate them. That's why it often puts up a fight, *resisting* any point of view that runs counter to its own cherished understanding of the world.

Fortunately, however, we have the power to overrule our story-self's objections. Not only is our brain able to grow new neurons and rewire itself, we can deliberately *direct* that rewiring though our own conscious effort, using the strategies we've covered throughout this book.

Of course, it takes considerable effort. The neural patterns that comprise our story-self are well entrenched, having been years in the making, many originating, as we've seen, prior to our ability to form conscious memories. To overcome our story-self's strong neural circuits, we must harness our weaker, less developed neural circuits in response, strengthening them in the process.

Mindfulness practices; the cultivation of awe, wonder, and gratitude; and the discipline of uncovering the unconscious attachments that fuel our resistances are all examples of "weaker circuits" we can bring to bear

To Resolve, Dissolve

I n my experience of surrendering, a space exists between letting go of the old neural pathways and the emergence of the new — an ever-so-brief moment in which it can feel as though we cease to exist, in which our sense of self dissolves and we're no longer sure of who we are or what we believe. People talk about that moment metaphorically as the "imaginal state"[1] — that stage in the chrysalis in which the form of the caterpillar literally dissolves so that it can later re-emerge as a butterfly.

I once had a particularly memorable experience of this metaphorical imaginal state. It came years ago, while helping my son with his homework.

He was in third grade and I was trying to help him with a math problem. He found it difficult and struggled to understand, and eventually he became frustrated, upset, and hard to talk to. Interestingly, as his emotions rose, I found mine did, too. I started to feel exasperated with him, angry, and was on the verge of "losing it."

Even in the midst of my emotion, however, I knew what was going on. When I was in third grade, I too had a hard time with math. My mother, an elementary school teacher, and my father, a mathematician, had little patience for my difficulties.

Their efforts to help me followed a set pattern: they'd get exasperated, then angry, and sometimes they would even end up slapping me for being so dense. It was, needless to say, a traumatic experience.

This old pattern of how my parents treated me wanted desperately to be repeated. I had internalized that negative energy, and now my story-self wanted to give my son what my parents had given me.

Armed with that piece of self-awareness, and harnessing what felt like enormous willpower, I instead chose a different path. I calmed down and suggested that we set the problem aside and come back to it later.

It might be hard to appreciate, but making that decision felt like a death of sorts to me. Those old neural patterns were so strong and so laden with emotion that they were desperate to burst forth. Surrendering left me free to make a different choice. Rather than acting from my story-self and giving my son what *I'd* been given, I was able to act from my unstory-self, giving him what I had *not* received: love.

He took my suggestion and we moved on to other homework. Fifteen minutes later, we came back to the math problem and sailed right through it. It was an incredible experience and an affirmation of the transformative power of surrender.

1   See https://www.scientificamerican.com/article/ caterpillar-butterfly-metamorphosis-explainer/.

as we learn to consciously participate in our brain's rewiring. All serve to activate our prefrontal cortex and promote its reintegration with our lower limbic structures — essential for regulating our emotional responses and maintaining response flexibility.

By integrating these practices into our life, we put our brain's synaptic symphony under a different conductor, one able to break free of the neural confines of our story-self so that new, better-integrated neural patterns can emerge. And with them, a more expansive and responsive sense of self.

WATCH

For a wonderful example of someone using his "weaker circuits" to overcome the stronger ones, check out this 3-minute perspective piece produced by the PBS Newshour. In it, novelist Akhil Sharma, a professor of literature at Rutgers University and a contributor to the *New Yorker* magazine, talks about his experience of "opening up to understand the experience of others."

You can find it on my Vimeo channel: https://vimeo.com/difficultconversations/. It's titled "Opening Up to Others."

Personal Assessment #5

Think again about your difficult conversation.

In this situation, what are you resisting?

- What would "surrender" look like? What would you be letting go of?
- Can you imagine what new options might emerge?
- Bonus question: what "weaker circuits" might you use to overcome the stronger ones?

1   Richard J. Davidson and Antoine Lutz, "Buddha's Brain: Neuroplasticity and Meditation," *IEEE Signal Processing Magazine* 25, no. 1 (September 2007), doi:10.1109/MSP.2008.4431873.

7

Integration

There is no self that will survive a real conversation.
There's no self that will survive a real meeting with
something other than itself. . . . And after a while, you
realize you actually don't want to keep that old static
identity. You want to move the pivot of your presence
from this thing you think is you into this meeting with
the future. . . . It's in this self-forgetfulness, where
you meet something other than yourself, that all kinds
of astonishing things happen.
— David Whyte, poet

Throughout this book, via the language of both science and metaphor, we've been talking about the importance of *integration* in working through our collective differences: in the language of science, the integration of our lower (limbic) and upper (neocortical) brain; and in the language of metaphor, the integration of our "story-" and "unstory-" selves.

Difficult conversations are a gymnasium in which we learn to master the art and science of integration. Difficult conversations ask us to set aside our filters and consider the world from another perspective. They ask us to listen to what we don't want to hear, and to acknowledge what we wish didn't exist. They ask us to embrace complexity, and to enlarge our circle of understanding.

They ask us, in other words, to "move the pivot" of our presence, to engage in conversation not as an isolated *I* focused on self-preservation, but as an integral *we* focused on mutual understanding and, potentially, mutual transformation.

Difficult conversations are difficult because they ask so much of us. But it's an essential ask, and a loving one, designed to further our personal and collective evolution. Remember: *interpersonal integration facilitates neural integration*. Every difficult conversation we navigate — every unconscious trigger made conscious, every negative projection withdrawn, every enemy made a friend — increases and strengthens our communities, our nation, and our world, and simultaneously, the connections between our upper and lower brain, making us evermore empowered agents of positive and healing change.

The three new survival strategies offered in this book — prioritizing the relationship over being right, seeing beyond our story, and transforming resistance into response — are heuristics to help us become such agents.

Each requires redefining or expanding our *I*— our sense of self — to make room for "the other," thereby unleashing our capacities for extraordinary creativity, resilience, compassion, generosity, responsiveness, and so much more.

At first, none of these strategies — reliant as they are on our "weaker circuits" — will come easily. It will take willpower and courage to put our *I* at risk, to let it encounter, with an open heart and open mind, something other than itself; to let it dissolve and then re-solve and then dissolve again — continuously shape-shifting into ever-more integrated, conscious, and responsive forms.

"The most difficult thing is the decision to act," Amelia Earhart is reported to have said. "The rest is merely tenacity."[1] Perhaps the mounting pressures we're under will make it easier for us to make decisions to act, for all the world's challenges, it seems, are now gathered at our doorstep. And every day they knock louder, demanding a response.

How we answer, and how we come to those answers, will affect the lives of generations to come. Will we retreat in fear and let the small-minded tribalism of our reptilian brain rule the day, or will we move forward with courage, our full, integrated humanity intact, and choose to work with others to build a more beautiful world — one we all know is possible?[2]

The choice, as always, is ours.

1 See https://www.ameliaearhart.com/.
2   A nod here to Charles Eisenstein's book *The More Beautiful World Our Hearts Know Is Possible.*

Afterword

This book is based on a workshop I've been facilitating around the country since the summer of 2017.

If you're interested in bringing the workshop to your organization or community, you can do this in one of two ways:

- You can invite me to lead a workshop in your community.
- You can lead a workshop yourself using materials I created, which include a detailed facilitator's guide. This do-it-yourself version has been developed as a series of weekly meetings, each about two hours in length.

To request either of these options, please contact me at: http://www.difficultconversationsproject.org/.

Appendix 1:
Stories of Transformation

Megan Phelps Roper's experience is far from the only example of what's possible when we prioritize the relationship over being right, see beyond our story, and transform resistance into response. If you look for them, stories abound of people doing the unexpected: reaching out to "the enemy" to create a new narrative of engagement and compassion over rejection and condemnation.

Following are summaries of three additional examples I came across while developing my workshop.

Michael Kent and Tiffany Whittier

Michael Kent, a committed neo-Nazi, had spent numerous years in and out of prison, the last time on drugs and weapons charges. But after being released in 2006, he caught a break that finally ended his cycle of incarceration: he was given a new case officer — a black woman named Tiffany Whittier.

Over the course of Michael's three-year probation, the pair formed an unlikely but close friendship. Unperturbed by his racist rhetoric and swastika tattoos — "that was his problem, not mine," she once told an interviewer — Tiffany connected with Michael by showing him acceptance and respect, two critical ingredients long absent from his life. Her approach had an impact. Michael's worldview began to change, eventually culminating in his decision to leave the neo-Nazi movement.

Asked by a reporter how she, a black woman, was able to look past Michael's racist worldview and have such a positive impact, Tiffany replied, "I'm not here to judge him. That's not my job. My job is to be that positive person in someone's life."

NOTE: *To learn more about Michael and Tiffany's story, see the* Washington Post *article "The 'Ironic' Friendship that Convinced a Former Neo-Nazi to Erase his Swastika Tattoos."*

Derek Black and Matthew Stevenson

Derek Black was born to be a white nationalist. His father, Don Black, had created the first — and, at the time, largest — white nationalist website. David Duke, the infamous former KKK Grand Wizard, was once married to Derek's mother, and was now Derek's godfather. Brought up with high hopes, Derek didn't disappoint. At age 10 he built a white nationalist website for children. And in his teens he not only attended and spoke at white nationalist rallies, he helped organize them. Bright and unusually articulate, Derek was regarded by many as the movement's future leader.

But when Derek entered the liberal New College in Florida, things began to change.

At first, he'd hoped to keep his white nationalist identity and activities secret, but that ended when a student stumbled across his writings on the Internet and shared them throughout the school community. The reaction was swift: the vast majority of Derek's classmates shunned him.

There was, however, one notable exception: Matthew Stevenson, an orthodox Jew, thought it was better to engage Derek than ostracize him, and so invited him to join his weekly Shabbat dinners at his campus apartment. Derek accepted, and that simple but courageous invitation began his transformation.

At first, the dinners were non-confrontational, avoiding any mention of white nationalism. But over time, as relationships were formed, they evolved into evenings of respectful yet challenging conversation about Derek's beliefs and actions. Derek, who had come to trust his new friends, began to listen and think in a new way, questioning his own white nationalist assumptions more deeply.

In 2013, shortly after graduating, he very publicly left the white nationalist movement, and he continues to speak out against it to this day.

NOTE: *To get Derek's full story, beautifully told, read* Rising Out of Hatred: The Awakening of a Former White Nationalist, *by Pulitzer Prize-winning author Eli Saslow. You can also read Saslow's 2016 article "The White Flight of Derek*

Black" in the Washington Post. *For podcast listeners, check out the interview with Derek and David, "How Friendship and Quiet Conversations Transformed a White Nationalist" through the podcast* On Being.

Daryl Davis and the KKK

Daryl Davis is a black rock 'n' roll musician with a strange hobby — he befriends members of the Ku Klux Klan. And while not a requirement, those friendships sometimes lead to surprising transformations: his KKK friends become *former* KKK members, turning over their hoods and robes to Daryl to add to his growing collection.

For Daryl, the seeds for this surprising avocation were planted as a child, when an early encounter with racism left him with a burning question: *How can they hate me if they don't even know me?*

By befriending members of the KKK, Daryl is giving them the opportunity to know him. His approach is controversial, and some say naïve, but in the last 30-plus years he's collected more than 200 robes, according to an NPR interview he gave in 2017.

In the same interview, Daryl described his approach this way:

When two enemies are talking, they're not fighting. It's when the talking ceases that the ground becomes fertile for violence. If you spend five minutes with your worst enemy — it doesn't have to be about race, it could be about anything —you will find that you both have something in common. As you build upon those commonalities, you're forming a relationship and as you build upon that relationship, you're forming a friendship. That's what would happen. I didn't convert anybody. They saw the light and converted themselves.

NOTE: To learn more about Daryl's approach and experiences, search on his name at TED.com. And to listen to Daryl's NPR interview, go to https://www.npr.org/programs/all-things-considered/2017/08/20/544882080. Daryl is also the subject of the documentary film Accidental Courtesy.

Appendix 2:

Why Should I?
The Power of Networks

One claim I've been making is that when we heal a relationship, we help heal our community, our nation, and even our world. And research by sociologists Nichols Christakis and James Fowler on the power of our social networks backs me up.

You've likely heard of the Six Degrees of Separation theory, which posits that there are at most six steps or "degrees of separation" between any two people. Less well known, but perhaps more important is what Christakis and Fowler call the Three Degrees of Influence theory: what we do and say ripples outward to influence the thoughts and behaviors of those within three degrees of us — "our friends (one degree), our friends' friends (two degrees), and even our friends' friends' friends (three degrees)."[1]

Of course, it doesn't stop there. The people within three degrees of us then influence the people within three degrees of them, and on it goes, our original impact rippling throughout our broader network. It's likely to even come back to us in some form, since within our network we can't help but be a friend of a friend of a friend influenced by what we first started. (Guess there's more truth than we thought to that old saying, "What goes around comes around"!)

But there's more. Christakis and Fowler make a distinction between what they call our network's strong and weak ties. Imagine a circle with a dot in the center. That dot is you. Your strong ties will be dots close to your own in the center, while your weak ties — those with whom you perhaps have less in common — are the dots further out on the circle's fringe.

What's interesting is that *it's at the fringe where our*

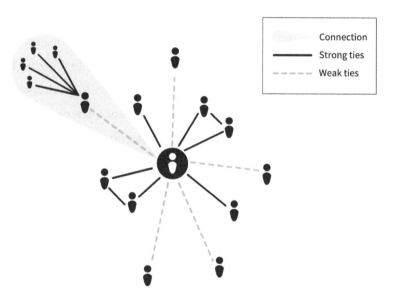

Our weak ties are at the fringe of our network. By cultivating our weak ties, we extend our connections and sphere of influence.

network is at its most creative and dynamic because it's those weak ties that serve as bridges to other people and groups with whom we're less likely to be in contact. By cultivating our weak ties, we extend our connections and sphere of influence well beyond our own close network.

This, as you can imagine, has important implications for healing our local, national, and even global divide. By building relationships with people with whom we disagree — by bringing them from outside our circle to at least its outer fringes — we leverage the power of the Three Degrees of Influence to produce an effect that ripples far beyond those particular individuals. In the words of Christakis and Fowler, "When we target the periphery of a network to help people reconnect, we help the whole fabric of society, not just [the] individuals at the fringe."[2]

1   Nicholas A. Christakis and James H. Fowler, *Connected: The Surprising Power of Our Social Networks and How They Shape Our Lives* (New York: Hachette Book Group, 2009), 28.
2   Ibid., 302.

Appendix 3:

Gratitude Practices

"Gratitude is happiness doubled by wonder," wrote author G.K. Chesterton. With those inspiring words in mind, below are three exercises to build your "gratitude muscles."

- **The Breath of Thanks.** Get settled and bring your attention to your breathing. Notice how your breath flows in and out without your having to do anything. Continue breathing in this way. For each of the next 5–8 exhalations, say the words thank you silently to remind yourself of the gift of your breath and how lucky you are to be alive.

- **The Gratitude Letter.** Think of someone who has been especially kind to you — a friend, a teacher, a coworker — whom you've never properly thanked. Write a letter thanking this person, being specific about what he or she did that affected your life. Then schedule a meeting, maybe over coffee or a drink, and deliver the letter in person. Don't tell the person what the meeting is about; let it be a surprise. This form of gratitude can have a long-lasting effect. One study showed that after writing and delivering a thank-you letter, people had increased levels of happiness even two months later.

- **The Gratitude Journal.** Take a few minutes every day to write down three things you're grateful for. To make it a better habit, try doing it at the same time every day. If you can't think of three things, write just one. If you can't think of even one thing, write, I'm grateful for the food I ate today or I'm grateful for the clothes I'm wearing. Even if a situation is 90 percent what you don't want, you can still be grateful for the other 10 percent.

Appendix 4:

End Well

Several weeks after taking my Difficult Conversations workshop, Lisa came up to me to tell me a success story. She'd shared some of the workshop content with her daughter, hoping that it would help her daughter deal with a difficult relationship she was having with her aunt. Her daughter took the advice, and the result, said Lisa, was little short of miraculous: after one conversation, the tension in their relationship dissolved.

Surprised and curious, I asked Lisa exactly what she'd shared with her daughter. I wanted to know how someone might distill an all-day workshop in a way that another person who was not there might actually find helpful. What Lisa told me I now consider a five-word distillation of the entire day:

Listen well and end well.

It's a brilliant summation. When we listen well to someone we're in conflict with, we're putting all three of our new survival strategies in operation. We're prioritizing the relationship, we're seeing beyond our story, and we're transforming resistance into response. Leave any one of those strategies out and — I'm convinced — true listening is impossible.

Ending well— concluding the conversation on a kind and gracious note, even if the conversation itself was heated — takes advantage of a powerful psychological dynamic: when an unpleasant experience has a happy ending, we tend to remember not just the ending, but the *whole event* more positively.

This was clearly illustrated in a study by psychologist Daniel Kahneman.[1] In his experiment, participants were asked to put one hand in ice-cold (57° F) water for 60 seconds. Afterward, they were asked to submerge their *other* hand in ice-cold water for 90 seconds, but with a twist: for the last 30 seconds, the temperature rose slightly, becoming two degrees warmer by the end of the additional 30-second period.

The rest you can probably guess: when the experimenters asked participants which trial they would choose to repeat if they had to, "nearly 70 percent of participants chose to repeat the 90-second trial, even though it involved 30 extra seconds of pain. Participants also said that the longer trial was less painful overall, less cold, and easier to cope with. Some even reported that it took less time."

So even if a conversation turns out to be particularly difficult or stressful, strive to end it well. As Celeste Headlee, author of *We Need to Talk,* puts it:

> It can be scary to talk about politics or religion with

someone else, so express your gratitude for their time and their openness. If you end the conversation in a friendly and gracious way, you set the groundwork and tone for future conversations.

1   Daniel Kahneman, Barbara L. Fredrickson, Charles A. Schreiber and Donald A. Redelmeier, "When More Pain Is Preferred to Less: Adding a Better End," *Psychological Science* 4, no. 6 (Nov. 1993), 401–405.

About the Author

KERN BEARE is a former Silicon Valley communications professional with deep roots in the fields of interpersonal communication and conflict resolution. He leads non-profit seminars and workshops on how to heal relationships and unleash our capacity for creative collaboration.

Kern's work in this field began in the 1980s, at the height of the Cold War, when he received a two-year fellowship from the Beyond War foundation, a fellowship that led to running educational programs on the obsolescence of war in the nuclear age and the imperative of learning to resolve conflict without violence. In the 1990s, Beyond War became the Foundation for Global Community, extending its mission to include social and environmental issues. He served on the board of the new organization and helped to develop an expanded offering of educational workshops.

In the early 2000s, Kern co-founded Global MindShift, a nonprofit enterprise that offered facilitated online workshops on the essential skills we need to survive and thrive in today's interconnected and interdependent world.

In 2016, following the U.S. Presidential election, Kern launched the Difficult Conversations Project, an initiative to help address our national divide. He now travels the country leading workshops based on the concepts in this book.

Kern holds a BA in psychology from the University of California at Los Angeles. He and his wife Amy have two grown sons — Joseph and Will — and live in Mountain View, California.

Made in United States
North Haven, CT
12 October 2021

10281672R10089